Praise for Findi

'*Finding Flourishing* masterfully blends biblical wisdom with the practical TIME framework, offering a simple yet profound strategy for improving wellbeing in relationships, work and personal growth. This book stands as a crucial guide for navigating the chaos of modern life, pointing readers towards fulfillment and flourishing through Jesus. It's an essential read for anyone on the path to personal transformation and a life marked by deep satisfaction and joy.'
Jordan Raynor, bestselling author of *The Sacredness of Secular Work* **and** *Redeeming Your Time*

'*Finding Flourishing* is a heartfelt, wise guide that feels like a breath of fresh air. It's not just a book; it's a journey through the ups and downs of life and relationships, grounded in spiritual truths. The author writes from personal experience, offering practical and relatable advice. Whether you're navigating parenthood, looking for better wellbeing, or figuring out relationships, this book meets you where you are with kindness and insight. If you're feeling overwhelmed by life, this book will help you find peace and a path toward a fuller, more meaningful life.'
Atinuke Awe, wife, mother of two and founder of Mums and Tea and Five X More

'Having had coaching sessions with Naomi, I have personally benefited from her deep wisdom and expertise in navigating work–life wellbeing from a faith perspective. The honest writing in *Finding Flourishing* is a breath of fresh-air, and provides a gentle, yet practical, framework for us to apply the principles to our own lives.'
Emma Borquaye, author and podcast host

'Written by a busy working mum who knows what she's talking about, *Finding Flourishing* combines practical advice and inspirational content. This book provides a great opportunity to pause, reflect and reorientate our lives around the things that really matter.'
Ruth Jackson, presenter, Premier Unbelievable, and mum to a boisterous toddler

'Naomi writes as a friend to anyone who is truly seeking to flourish. She meets the reader where they are, but brings… a depth and richness that can only come from a tenacious excavation and application of truth in her own life. I am thankful for her work and the empathy available to us all in this book, which encourages us with stories, practical instruction and truth to truly flourish no matter what the season.'
Susanna Wright, writer and filmmaker

'A beautiful, gentle reminder of profound truth. Putting into perspective faith and wellbeing, drawing on scripture written many years ago yet that are still so relevant for today's struggles, bringing peace, comfort and encouragement. Naomi has an honest yet kind tone… you almost feel like you are in conversation with an old friend over tea. From the faith focus to food for thought prompts, this really is a book, journal and a friend in one. A timely piece of work that is so needed in the wellbeing space and I know will equip anyone who reads it with the tools and encouragement to flourish.'
Yasmin Elizabeth-Mfon, creative consultant and founder of Pick Me Up Inc

'Naomi expertly debunks the myth of work–life balance and urges us towards a much healthier, and more obtainable, "wellbeing" goal instead. I was worried that the book would give me yet more to add to my already full "to-do" list but instead it made me feel seen, understood and empowered to make changes. This well researched book could be a lifeline for many struggling to keep up with expectations from themselves and/or others. I thoroughly recommend it.'
Loretta Andrews, music manager and artist development coach

'This book is a gift into the world. The stories, the level of relatability and authenticity mixed with the invitation to take what you have read and integrate it into your everyday, ordinary, busy life makes this book not only readable but actionable too. Thank you Naomi for guiding your readers towards wellbeing. This is now my go-to gift for the women in my life.'
Jo Hargreaves, The Faith Filled Therapist

'Naomi is such a leader, not only in talking about wellbeing and finding your unique time and pace – but in living it and demonstrating to others as well. With her guidance, I've found systems that have helped me flourish and find peace in the busyness of life. I'm so excited that now, her message gets to reach thousands of new people. Dive into the book and get ready to feel refreshed and renewed!'
Abiola Babarinde, brand strategist and wellbeing enthusiast

'Naomi Aidoo presents a compelling blend of faith and practical wisdom, offering readers a roadmap to navigate the complexities of modern life with grace and purpose. Through insightful reflections on wellbeing and relationships, mindset and the transformative TIME framework, this book provides not just inspiration, but tangible steps toward everyday flourishing. I highly recommend this book to anyone seeking to align their life with timeless biblical principles while flourishing in their work and relationships.'
Steve Cockram, cofounder of GiANT

'Naomi brings thoughtful reflections, coaching wisdom and practical advice together to encourage everyone to invest in their wellbeing. It's a valuable resource.'
Rachael Newham, theology of mental health specialist and author

BRF Ministries

15 The Chambers, Vineyard
Abingdon OX14 3FE
brf.org.uk | +44 (0)1865 319700

Bible Reading Fellowship is a charity (233280)
and company limited by guarantee (301324),
registered in England and Wales

ISBN 978 1 80039 274 8
First published 2024
10 9 8 7 6 5 4 3 2 1 0
All rights reserved

Acknowledgements
Unless otherwise acknowledged, scripture quotations are taken from The Holy Bible,
New International Version (Anglicised edition) copyright © 1979, 1984, 2011 by Biblica.
Used by permission of Hodder & Stoughton Publishers, a Hachette UK company. All
rights reserved. 'NIV' is a registered trademark of Biblica. UK trademark number 1448790.
Scripture quotations marked ESV: The Holy Bible, English Standard Version, published by
HarperCollins Publishers, © 2001 Crossway Bibles, a division of Good News Publishers. Used
by permission. All rights reserved.

Every effort has been made to trace and contact copyright owners for material used in
this resource. We apologise for any inadvertent omissions or errors, and would ask those
concerned to contact us so that full acknowledgement can be made in the future.

A catalogue record for this book is available from the British Library

Printed and bound by CPI Group (UK) Ltd, Croydon CR0 4YY

Finding Flourishing

Time and pace for your work-life wellbeing

Naomi Aidoo

BRF
Ministries

Also available as an audiobook narrated by Naomi Aidoo. A perfect companion for the commute, the walk home after dropping the kids at school, you-time at the gym or a bed-time listen.

To my husband, James: thank you for everything seen and unseen. Your commitment to us finding flourishing will always mean more than I can articulate.

To my children, Micah and Neriah: may you always find flourishing in he who formed you.

Contents

Introduction 11

1 Wellbeing and relationships 23

2 Wellbeing and hope 35

3 Wellbeing and our mindset 45

4 Wellbeing and the TIME framework: an introduction 55

5 Wellbeing and our goals (E) 67

6 Wellbeing and gratitude (T) 79

7 Wellbeing and productivity (I) 89

8 Wellbeing and real self-care (M) 101

Wellbeing over well-balanced: concluding reflection 113

Notes 117

Journal pages 118

Introduction

The room was pitch black, and as I rocked my ten-month-old baby to sleep for the umpteenth time that night, while trying to make sure I didn't accidentally tread on the creaky floorboard and wake up my eldest, who was sleeping soundly, I found myself crying out to God (silently, of course).

'How, and why, am I someone who is supposed to write a book about wellbeing?'

Here I was, a mum of two very young children, one of whom still wasn't sleeping through the night, and I honestly felt like I had nothing to give. I had scattered fragments I'd collected over the years, which I absolutely knew had been useful to me and to others. But standing, shushing, swaying into the early hours of the morning with a baby in my arms certainly didn't feel like the persona or impression I wanted to give to the world when I spoke about work–life wellbeing. 'Aren't I meant to be an expert of sorts or, at the very least, have everything together and not be sleeping in three-hour chunks night after night?' I silently asked myself.

We see the wellbeing gurus, don't we? Well-rested, well-nourished and well-presented. Standing in my children's bedroom at 1.00 am that night, I felt like a fraud. That is until God stepped in, as he so often does, and graciously reminded me of the truth:

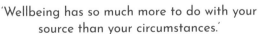

'Wellbeing has so much more to do with your
source than your circumstances.'

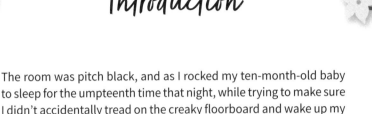

The balm that these words provided was, without my knowing it, exactly what I needed. I had no other source but God. I'd tried others and undoubtedly found them wanting.

Although God was absolutely my source – of faith, strength, hope, joy, peace and everything in between – I could easily recall seasons of my life where I'd felt much closer to him than I did that night; days where I'd poured over my Bible for hours as opposed to in bite-size, interrupted chunks; days where I'd led Bible studies and large online communities; days where sleep featured more heavily, and my time was more my own.

Despite receiving this word about my source outweighing my circumstances, I stalled in beginning to write the book you're now holding for a few more months. I didn't want to admit it then, but I think I simply thought that I'd soon feel how I used to feel 'back then', and I'd then be the expert required to write a manuscript which mattered.

Time marched on, as it does. I worked a little more with my daughter in the area of sleep, and she started sleeping through the night. My son started school. And still I waited.

For anyone who's experienced any form of life alteration, such as having a child, you'll know that who you once were and who you've now become are quite different people. There's an excitement about the new alongside a longing for what once was. I'd felt this four years prior when my eldest was born, and it had crept back in when faced with the magnitude of writing something I wanted other people to learn and benefit from. 'If I could just be who I used to be,' I thought, 'then I wouldn't feel so under-qualified.' But God's words continued to ring true – this was about my source and not my circumstances. And the same is to be said for you.

Who or what is your source? When you consider that your wellbeing could be found there, does that leave you wanting?

Finding Flourishing is a book in which I'm delighted to share a different perspective on work–life wellbeing: a perspective which doesn't automatically assume you've got everything together and just need a few tweaks, nor place unrealistic expectations on your time. Instead *Finding Flourishing* will serve you with a reminder of your humanness, with an understanding that your humanness is not a shock to God, and with tools which will enable you to keep going and keep growing in your own time and at your own pace.

What *Finding Flourishing* will and won't do

If at one end of the spectrum there is me in my mid-30s, rocking my baby in a pitch-black room in the dead of night, at the other end is me in my early 20s.

At 21, I was nearing the end of one of the most transformative years of my life on a gap year with my church. Among various types of work within the community, I'd had the privilege of working within local schools leading assemblies and PSHE lessons. It was during those times that I knew whatever 'next' looked like for me, I wanted it to include working with young people.

A year or so later, I'd qualified as a teacher and was working in a school notorious for its challenges. So much so, in fact, that it was deemed inadequate by OFSTED during my training year and was then taken over and granted academy status the following year in an attempt to turn it around. As tumultuous as this sounds, I actually enjoyed the challenge and soon realised that the students I most enjoyed working with were indeed the ones deemed 'challenging'.

During the day-to-day routine of those years, I set up initiatives such as lunchtime groups and after-school activities, which meant that students who were notorious for being in school only for the hours absolutely necessary found themselves lingering behind and engaging with what was there for them to do. In a lot of ways, knowing I was having an impact in this way was hugely rewarding, and I kept increasing the amount I was doing in this area. At one point, I was running multiple youth-work provisions after school with my church, alongside my full-time job as a teacher.

However, I soon learned the hard way that just because something is good, that doesn't mean you shouldn't place boundaries around it. I took my work too far and became burnt out, all in the name of 'calling' and passion. Suddenly, getting out of bed was harder than it used to be, and I was often tearful for what I felt was no reason. A lack of boundaries and really listening to myself led to an inability to do the things which months earlier had felt like second nature.

After a trip to the doctor, I was diagnosed with moderate depression and anxiety and prescribed a pot of pills. Thankfully, this wasn't a permanent position for me, but that diagnosis in my early 20s serves as a reminder for me personally of where burnout can lead.

When I was able to evaluate what needed to change and had the capacity to do so, I gradually started ensuring that boundaries and better habits were in place, as well as giving myself space to ask myself questions about how I was doing at at any given time, which I usually did through my journal. This led to wellbeing becoming much more of a prominent feature in my life and work, and was therefore something which I ensured that later my coaching clients paid attention to within themselves as well.

With my background in teaching rather than medicine, the thoughts and tools this book will equip you with are not intended to be diagnostic. Although I will certainly discuss mental health, both from research and from my own as well as others' experience, and I trust this will be beneficial, I am not a doctor. It's important to emphasise from the very beginning, that despite what you might have been told, there's no shame or embarrassment in seeking medical support for issues which need medical attention. Quite the opposite, in fact.

Operating from my current position as a coach, however, it's important to state that I will ask questions! These will be questions that I've asked myself, questions which will ask you to truly search yourself and your circumstances and cause you to assess the gap between where you are and where you want to be – never from a place of condemnation or criticism, but rather to gain clarity and momentum for what's next. *Finding Flourishing* will offer you journal prompts and questions for reflection which are designed to give meaningful momentum.

Whether you're currently feeling blissful or burnt out, *Finding Flourishing* aims to meet you there. All it requires from you is some honesty, which might not always feel comfortable, but will lead to both subtle and significant shifts.

What is wellbeing?

To summarise these introductory thoughts on wellbeing, let's visit Abraham Maslow and his famous hierarchy of needs (1943) for a moment. Maslow suggested that human beings have both deficiency needs (D needs) and being needs (B needs). The deficiency needs are split into four categories, moving from the most basic need to the more complex; physiological; safety; love and belonging; and self-esteem. The B need is 'self-actualisation' and Maslow argued that, when the D needs are 'more or less met', our natural disposition is to seek to fill that growth and being need of self-actualisation, which of course, is never truly met as we continue to go and grow in the direction of our destination.

Wellbeing can be defined as a state of being comfortable, healthy or happy. The broad nature of this definition leaves a lot of room for interpretation, and rightly so. One person's comfort might look different to another's and, if we're to think seriously about Maslow's hierarchy of needs, we'd be highly presumptuous to suggest that doing X will instantly change our lives. Each individual needs different types of care and support in order to truly thrive.

This is why wellbeing isn't something we can just add to our to-do list, as though we can simply tick a box to show that we've meditated for the ten minutes we were supposed to today. I don't believe it's somewhere we arrive and stay at; rather it's somewhere we're con-tinually re-seeking as our external circumstances shift and change. While our circumstances aren't the be all and end all for wellbeing, how we're currently experiencing life is often a significant factor in the outlook we possess at any given point, and it's important to con-tinue to make enquiries there. Indeed, we must look inward in order to avoid plastering toxic productivity or positivity over something much more than skin deep.

Wellbeing over well-balanced?

Both in and outside of the wellbeing arena, we hear the phrase 'work–life balance'. While I understand the sentiment, as a busy working mum of two, I don't think 'balance' truly exists for a lot of people, and the apparent lack of it in our often full-to-the-brim lives can cause us to feel guilty or to think that we're doing something wrong by not obtaining it.

Now, before you think that *Finding Flourishing* is all about how work-ing hard is evil and that we should all just chill out a bit and leave our email 'out of office' message permanently on, that's not what I mean. In fact, this is part of the reason that I think the notion of work–life balance is impractical. It suggests that all of the plates should be perfectly and simultaneously spinning and that dropping any one of them at any given point means you've failed.

So no, I don't hold to the popular belief that it is a problem if someone wants to 'burn the midnight oil' for a few weeks in a row while working on a busy project. I think it's counterproductive to force someone to 'just stop' while they're in the midst of some major work. I'm sure you know as well as I do that sometimes you're just 'in the flow' and you don't notice the hours whiz by as your blank page *finally* fills up with words.

The professional networking site LinkedIn now includes 'stay-at-home parent' in the list of job titles on their site. (I'm aware there were a lot of mixed responses about whether or not to use this based on what potential employers might think, but that's another story for another day.) I think this is fantastic and recognises that raising children, though not paid employment, is still work. Even acknowledging this to yourself can help you realise that your time spent raising children was not 'doing nothing', but was productivity happening in a different way to the method typically prescribed.

Similarly, I don't think there's much of an issue if, after one of those particularly busy periods of non-stop work or raising little people, you have a few weeks/months/whatever period of time is needed when you're not 'go, go, go' and you actually sit back and take it a little easy… or easier.

If work–life balance exists, I think it comes in waves which last weeks and months, even years; it's not something you have to ensure you have every day.

Yes, make sure you go to the bathroom and eat a meal during the busy seasons, and make sure you take a shower and pick the laundry up off of the floor during your more chilled ones. But let's not make the way we live our day-to-day lives clinical, robotic and full of 'should'. Instead, let's remind ourselves that we're human beings and not human doings. *Finding Flourishing* is a book which will help you do just that.

Faith focus

Along with journal prompts and questions for reflection, each chapter of *Finding Flourishing* will include a 'Faith focus'. As a Christian, I firmly believe that God has a lot to say about wellbeing, both generally and for each of us specifically. He cares about human flourishing. For one reason or another, wellbeing isn't something which is often spoken about at church, and this in itself can cause people, at best, to question whether it's a topic God has any interest in. At worst, it can cause us to believe that God is actually against us thinking about wellbeing at all. When a theme or a topic is commonly coined as personal development or 'self-help', it can instantaneously be incorrectly thought that God wants nothing to do with it. Our chapter-by-chapter 'Faith focus' will aim to shed light on what God might say pertaining to wellbeing. If, as I heard that night while rocking my daughter, wellbeing has much more to do with our source than our circumstances, it would be irresponsible of me to include methods, hacks and frameworks here while leaving no room for God's perspective. Although these thoughts won't be exhaustive, I do hope they'll give you space to reflect biblically.

I've been interested in wellbeing generally for a long time and for most of this duration I've specifically found myself thinking about it through a faith perspective. Before I became a coach and worked in my own business full-time, I worked part-time for my church and often found myself thinking about initiatives and ways in which we as the church leadership team could encourage more openness both from and for members of the congregation whose day-to-day lives had very little to do with typical 'church ministry'. One of the suggestions I gave (which didn't go ahead in the end, due to an already packed schedule!) was 'Well Church', which essentially was about people taking time to pause and recognise that they were fully and wholly seen by Jesus, no matter what their circumstances. It would have been space for people to share, to be prayed for and to walk away knowing that the idea people can come to church 'as they are' isn't theoretical, but real. Although this might not have improved their circumstances on the spot, it would have started that journey, even by way of a realisation that life in Jesus could look different to anything else they'd been trying. The inspiration behind this initiative was a story found in John 4.

John 4:1–42 documents a story often referred to as 'The woman at the well'. The story opens with Jesus on a journey and verse 4 indicates that he 'had to go through Samaria'. Although geographically this was the logical route to take, strict Jews wouldn't take it in order to avoid defilement from the Samaritans. In the story, an unnamed Samaritan woman happens to be drawing water from a well at the hottest point of the day; she was guaranteed some privacy as no one else would be drawing water at this time, preferring the cooler morning or evening shift. This way, she could avoid the judgemental stares. As we head back to this 'had to' phrase, it begins to tell us so beautifully that Jesus meets us where we're at. He could have taken the longer but more 'appropriate' route to Galilee, but he 'had to' meet this woman.

The story goes on to illustrate so clearly that Jesus knows and sees every aspect of our lives, even the parts we're ashamed of. This woman had been leading a promiscuous life. However, rather than drawing attention to this and shaming her for her circumstances, Jesus gently steers and guides her into realising that her source – perhaps a need for affirmation and affection – wasn't the right place to keep going to. He awakens her to the fact that true life is in him. He uses the metaphor of drawing water from the well by describing himself, and indeed, the Holy Spirit to come, as 'living water', a source which will never run dry. As he did with this woman, when Jesus reminds us of the significance of our source, putting our trust in him as opposed to our circumstances, it causes us to think and therefore do differently.

Our 'Faith focus' will reflect on God's perspective on each of the themes *Finding Flourishing* explores, providing you with a view you otherwise might not have considered.

Food for thought

Each chapter of *Finding Flourishing* will also feature questions and prompts, which will cause you to think about what you've read and then, when you're ready and when it's relevant, to apply some of what you've learned to your life. So, as we journey through the rest of the book, here are some initial questions to get you thinking:

1 What or whom do you consider to be your 'source'? When you consider your wellbeing as having much more to do with this than with your circumstances, does this serve as encouragement, or not?

2 What stage of life do you think or know that you're currently in, and what are you trying to squeeze into it from a place of 'should', because you feel like you're supposed to, rather than taking heed of where you're currently at and acting accordingly?

3 What have your previous thoughts been about wellbeing and God (if any)? Have these changed over time, or are you willing to think about this area a little differently as you go through *Finding Flourishing*?

1

Wellbeing and relationships

As my friend, almost a decade younger than myself, spoke to me, wondering why she was not yet married with children, her words reminded me very much of my own. I'd had the same conversations at about the same stage she was at. Longing for a family while being surrounded by so many who appeared to have that dream fulfilled was certainly one of my hardest waits. I remember being a brides-maid several times before I was a bride. Each time, dealing with the conflicting emotions of utter joy for my friend paired with the dull ache of longing for what was yet to be mine.

The conversation with my friend moved quickly though to her recent pursuits – learning to teach English as a second language and study-ing New Testament Greek, to name just two. I felt a familiar pang. A pang which reminded me of the things I didn't have the time to take on because of my family commitments alongside writing and working and cleaning and… well, you get the idea. This conversation had highlighted the fact that I couldn't just pick up an extra course or two at this stage of life without something else having to give. These were things, however, which I had found myself free and able to do during the aforementioned time of longing. I'm sure the emotion I felt during this fleeting conversation was the same pang my friend might feel when one of my children calls me 'Mama', or my husband puts his arm around my shoulders.

Sometimes we find ourselves in seasons when we are near constantly surrounded by those we're in close relationship with, perhaps while raising young children or caring for an elderly or infirm relative. In these moments, we may long for some silence and solitude. Yet, during those times when we've experienced much more silence and solitude than we have togetherness, the noise of young children charging around the house and the frantic nature of the school run, or the quiet comfort we once had even in the sometimes sadness of caring for a loved one at the end of their life, might be exactly what we seek. The lack of it might leave us longing.

We can so often feel this pang when faced with the reality of what we *don't* have – the pang of comparison. All too often, we can overlook what we have been granted in this period and long for what our neighbour or our friend has.

How often have you scrolled through social media and looked upon both those you know and those you don't with *some* kind of pre-formed opinion? Something which causes you to decide how you'll respond to that person, if at all? How much of this type of thought process translates beyond the internet to when we find ourselves face to face with others, heads full of preconceived ideas formed on the basis of very little information? The relationships we have with others will certainly be built on a pretty rocky foundation if we're always viewing them through the lens of comparison or even envy. When we approach our relationships from a place of neutrality, we grow them without agenda or bias. I believe that much of what helps us to do this is a sense of comfort, acceptance and love of ourselves.

Alongside thinking about wellbeing in light of our relationships with others, we'll also go inwards and think about the relationship we have with ourselves, because the two, of course, go hand in hand.

Digging deeper

Throughout Genesis 1, God speaks of his creation as *tôb*, which is the Hebrew word for 'good', also rendered as 'beautiful', 'best' and even 'bountiful'. The concluding verse of the chapter goes on to say that 'God saw all that he had made, and it was very good' (Genesis 1:31). It is then in Genesis 2:18 that God states the very first thing that isn't good, and that's for man to be alone, to be outside of relationship with others.

Of course, Adam wasn't actually alone. Later, in Genesis 3:8, we read that God walked in the garden he had created and it therefore wouldn't be a stretch too far to assume that God was also walking in the garden back when it was just Adam who inhabited it with him. And yet, despite God's presence, he still knew that Adam needed a *person*, a companion to walk side by side with him.

We don't read that Adam himself felt this loneliness; we don't see any indication that he asked God for someone to help him. Instead, we see an omniscient God knowing exactly what his creation needed before the man could even recognise or see this for himself. This should give us great comfort and hope for today. God sees. God knows. God acts.

The Bible continually emphasises the importance of relationships. From God creating both man and woman (Genesis 2), to Esther and her uncle Mordecai coming up with a plan to save an entire nation (Esther 4), to four friends bringing their paralysed friend to Jesus (Matthew 9:1–8), to Jesus himself choosing twelve trusted disciples to walk and journey with him (Matthew 10:2), it's plain to see that isolation was never God's idea when it comes to how we do life.

For this chapter's 'Faith focus', we'll land in the book of 1 Corinthians 12:12–31. As we continue to explore the variety of ways in which our relationships will have a bearing on our wellbeing, both positively and negatively, we'll use these verses to explore how essential we are to and for each other.

How and why are relationships linked to wellbeing?

So much of the wellbeing space now is linked to *self*-realisation, *self*-actualisation and *self*-worth. While these factors are important when we consider this conversation, they miss the depth and beauty of how wellbeing can flourish against the backdrop of our relationships.

The Mental Health Foundation has coined a phrase for relationships as 'the forgotten foundation of mental health and wellbeing'. This notion certainly steers us away from the idea that true wellbeing is found in separation and isolation. In light of the pandemic years, I think we all appreciate more than ever how crucial connectedness is. However, our theoretical understanding of something and our ability to put into practice what we've understood are two very different things.

The findings of one piece of research, which collated 148 studies, indicated that 'the influence of social relationships on the risk of death are comparable with well-established risk factors for mortality such as smoking and alcohol consumption and exceed the influence of other risk factors such as physical inactivity and obesity'.[1]

Flexible working has opened up so many fantastic opportunities for more autonomous work and for working within global teams. These are circumstances that I, as an introvert, have greatly benefited from and wouldn't choose to trade for the commute and classroom of my former working life. However, I can certainly confess to times of being perhaps a little too comfortable within the confines of my own home. While there's nothing inherently wrong with that, I have undoubtedly found myself at times, for want of a better term, less comfortable with the world around me after particularly extended times of keeping myself to myself. This is the type of isolation I believe God said wasn't good back in Genesis, and still says isn't good now.

By ourselves, we have less space for accountability, support, friendship and even challenging conversations, which go on to shape us. I remember strongly relating to a quote I once read, which said something like, 'I'm the nicest person ever before 8.00 am, and then everyone else wakes up!' It's relatively easy to maintain our peace and poise when there's no one around us to frustrate, annoy or distract us or to try our patience. But in having that, we lose so much more – love and care, support and back-up, accountability and sanctification, which we'll explore a little more shortly. It is not good for man (or woman, of course) to be alone.

Relationship with self

As I alluded to earlier in the chapter, so much about our relationships with others is linked to our relationship with ourselves. From the way we steward our time, to how we maintain healthy boundaries with others, there's so much to explore from the point of view of 'self'. One of the assumptions I've found, particularly among Christians, is that ignoring our own needs and instead focusing on everyone and everything above ourselves is actually the way we *should* live. Now yes, the Bible talks about the fact we should 'honour one another' (Romans 12:10) and deny ourselves (Matthew 16:24–26). However, it is also pretty clear on our need to love our neighbour *as we love ourselves* (Matthew 22:39).

When we take that perspective, how comfortable would we feel about loving our nearest and dearest with the love we love ourselves with? Would the words which speak negativity ('I'm so stupid', 'Why do

I always do stuff like that?', etc.) be the sort of words we'd feel happy speaking over our children, for example? Of course they wouldn't. And yet so many of us are our own harshest critics; we can be all too ready to offer to others advice and empathy that we struggle to clothe ourselves with.

When our relationship with ourselves is skewed, it can absolutely do the same to our relationships with one another. Without keeping in check any of the jealousy, anger or bitterness we find ourselves facing when we look at those around us, we can unintentionally bring those elements into our relationships with one another and hold a particular view on those we're meant to love, purely because of the way in which we're viewing ourselves.

So what does it mean to love ourselves without becoming so self-obsessed and self-absorbed that we forget the fact we were never meant to do life alone? Again, Jesus models it better than I could ever explain it:

> Yet the news about him spread all the more, so that crowds of people came to hear him and to be healed of their illnesses. But Jesus often withdrew to lonely places and prayed. One day Jesus was teaching, and Pharisees and teachers of the law were sitting there. They had come from every village of Galilee and from Judea and Jerusalem. And the power of the Lord was with Jesus to heal those who were ill.
> LUKE 5:15–17

Jesus' ministry at this point was at its peak. He was continually healing, teaching and preaching. There didn't appear to be any need too great for him to meet. And the need for Jesus from the people around him at this point was great indeed, but this didn't cause him to drop everything and lose sight of his own needs at any given moment. His selfless and humble nature didn't bend and break at the whim of the crowd. People-pleasing was not required in order for him to live out his purpose. And people-pleasing is a big one, isn't it? It's built within us to want to impress, whether that be our family and friends, our colleagues or our bosses. Almost all of us will have faced this innate desire to 'prove' ourselves worthy of something, even if that apparent proof of worth only lies in receiving the applause and accolades of those we're seeking it from.

These verses tell us that Jesus was completely clear on his mission and purpose, and because of that, he knew what he would and wouldn't be available for. They don't tell us that the need had died down, which meant he could finally catch a break. In fact, they state that the news about him actually spread more, and therefore more and more people came to him for help. Fully divine and yet somehow fully man, Jesus could have done it all. However, he chose not to. We're told in verse 16 that Jesus *often* withdrew from the crowds in order to spend some time praying. What's more, he didn't even try to respond to the crowds when they pressed in and wanted more than he was willing to give at that point. How often have we been met with a need we think we 'should' meet, despite feeling as though we are completely spent in terms of our own capacity? How often do we push ourselves and, in doing so, feel resentful and annoyed about it? Sometimes, when we're clear on what we say 'no' to, it can make our 'yes' all the more significant.

Beyond boundaries alone, though, it's key to indicate here *why* Jesus took the time away that he did. He withdrew to pray to his Father. This was the most important relationship he had, and as Christians, it's the most important one we have too. So often when we're at the end of our own resources, we can withdraw to complain, grumble or ignore. The next time we don't feel we can go on, whatever the circumstance might be, what if we were to consider praying about it before complaining to a coworker (who will likely agree with you and further fuel the fire of frustration). Prayer changes us and changes our perspective.

In verse 17, we read of Jesus teaching people who had come from 'every village of Galilee and from Judea and Jerusalem'. It also indicates that he was filled with power to heal, which he indeed goes on to do. Having clarity and certainty about what his purpose was meant that Jesus was also clear on how intentional he needed to be with rest, solitude and prayer if he was to have the strength and ability to fulfil it.

Relationships throughout the seasons

When I find time to head to cafes to work for a change of scenery, as opposed to my desk at home, I lap up the opportunity. Despite the fact that I'm often sitting there with my earbuds in and am very much keeping to myself, there's something about the connectedness I feel when I'm working alongside others who are chatting, laughing and working too.

On one occasion, I was typing away when I overheard a conversation between a group of women who appeared to be in their 50s and 60s. One of the women introduced two members of the group to one another and when one asked how the other two knew each other, their response came as a pleasant surprise. 'NCT group,' they said. The National Childbirth Trust (NCT) is the UK's largest charity providing information and support in pregnancy and early parenthood. My husband and I were part of an NCT group when I was pregnant with my eldest. These women went on to talk about their children, who were now in their 20s and 30s, and I couldn't help but smile. The unity and bond I have with some of my friends now, who are also in the throes of parenthood, is certainly something special. Being able to talk about anything from baby bowel movements to behaviour is unique.

There's something about seasons of significance which shape you, isn't there? The relationships around you during those seasons are often of utmost importance too. One of my friends today is someone

I met when I was first exploring faith for myself as a teenager; another I met when I'd just started my teaching career and was at my very first school, navigating the trials and triumphs of my first 'proper' job. I truly believe that God puts people in our path during the different seasons and stages of our lives for good reason – so that we can be blessed, and indeed be a blessing. With that, let's conclude this chapter with our main 'Faith focus'.

Faith focus: 'One body, many parts'

Paul begins 1 Corinthians 12 talking about spiritual gifts and how people are given different types of gifts. After this, he goes on to describe the body as a metaphor for the church. Interestingly, when first speaking about specific body parts, Paul mentions a foot claiming that it's not a part of the body because it's not a hand. He concludes that this declaration wouldn't make the foot any less a part of the body at all. This recalls the comparison element of being in relationships mentioned earlier.

Paul emphasises this point with another two body parts and states in verse 17: 'If the whole body were an eye, where would the sense of hearing be? If the whole body were an ear, where would the sense of smell be?' The point he's driving here is clear: without one another, we don't function as we ought to. However, just like ourselves now, in our individualistic and often self-centred society, the Corinthians clearly needed the same reminders.

In verse 21, Paul remarks that an eye cannot simply say to a hand, to the head or to the feet that they have no need of each other, and he mentions, in fact, the special honour that parts which seem weaker need to be given; those parts are actually indispensable. In our culture of 'hustle' and 'grind', it can be easy to give accolades and admiration only to those who appear to be doing it all. How often have we dismissed the contributions of those who are less like us than the people we're more comfortable relating to and taking soundings from?

The entirety of this section of 1 Corinthians 12 is both a stark reminder and a reality check regarding the relationships we have with each other. Yes, there are differences in a multitude of areas and, yes, it may even be the case that some possess more than others do, whether that be materially or in terms of position and power. But in spite of that, one thing is clear: difference is absolutely not meant to equal denial. Just as God spoke in Genesis, it isn't good for us to be alone. What's more, being together, both with those we find it more challenging to be with and those we could spend hours with non-stop, actually enriches and develops us more than we know.

Food for thought

1 Thinking about your relationship with yourself, have you 'made peace' with your current season of life? What are you actively doing to a) fully embrace and enjoy it, and b) remove the temptation to compare your lot with someone else's?

2 When you think about that current season, based on the question above, what sort of physical, mental and spiritual practices are required for you to maintain yourself in the midst of all you give?

3 What part of 1 Corinthians 12 do you find most difficult to comprehend? Why do you think this is, and what can you do to challenge this way of thinking?

2

Wellbeing and hope

At the beginning of a coaching programme with a new client or group, I use a well-known tool called 'The Wheel of Life' in order to assess and understand where a person is at currently, both in their life and their work. This tool asks people to rank their emotions and current experience according to a particular theme. There are many different variations of 'The Wheel of Life', and it's typically up to the practitioner to decide which themes they want their clients to explore based on the nature of the coaching experience they're facilitating for them. As 'work–life wellbeing' is the typical foundation for my coaching, one of the eight themes I explore through the use of 'The Wheel of Life' is hope.

I have found the presence of the notion of hope in these sessions to be hugely impactful. It's the theme which is undoubtedly most commented on and typically explored to the greatest extent. People are intrigued by and invested in hope.

Hope has a wide range of definitions and, depending on what circles you move in, can get both good and bad press. Hope is paramount to wellbeing because without it we can find ourselves despairing, which, in the long run, does nothing for anyone. If we, individually or collectively, want to get somewhere or accomplish something, hope is fundamental to us doing so, because sometimes it will feel like we want to give up.

One way I like to describe wellbeing is as 'holistic health, hope and happiness, which reflects and acts on the past, present and future'. This idea, and the use of the word 'hope' within it, has been shaped and moulded as I've worked with clients. With some clients, their ranking for most other aspects on the wheel can be low for one reason or another, and yet hope still receives the highest score. Supporting clients to simply witness this fact can be a catalyst in the momentum they gain thereafter. Even an acknowledgement that there's hope for the future in the midst of otherwise difficult times can be enough to mobilise action and motivate change.

American writer and politician Clare Boothe Luce (1903–87) said: 'There are no hopeless situations; there are only people who have grown hopeless about them.' This is a quote I profoundly resonate with in light of the importance of hope and its connectedness to wellbeing. If our wellbeing is much more dependent on our source than it is on our circumstances, hope is of the utmost importance. What we hope in, and why we hope in it, will also have a bearing on how robust this strategy actually is, which we'll explore within our 'Faith focus'. However, perhaps surprisingly, hope is of huge value and importance in and of itself too.

Digging deeper

As a Christian, my hope is undoubtedly rooted in Jesus and the sure foundation that a life in him provides. This isn't dependent on my circumstances, but it also doesn't ignore the fact that some circumstances can be hard, even devastating. Jesus doesn't overlook this at any point either.

In John's gospel, Jesus says: 'The thief comes only to steal and kill and destroy; I have come that they may have life, and have it to the full' (John 10:10). Jesus' desire and intention is abundant life for us today. But how can this be possible when even the most privileged of people don't live a life devoid of problems? More significantly, how can this be possible when so many across the globe face war, famine, poverty and worse? Some of this will be answered in the aforementioned verse. Death and destruction were never part of God's will; they're very much the plan and attack of the enemy. However, these things are also not a shock to God. He's not taken aback by horrific circumstances. Also in John's gospel, Jesus says: 'I have told you these things, so that in me you may have peace. In this world you will have trouble. But take heart! I have overcome the world' (16:33). Trouble in this life is promised, and yet it seems as though life to the full is also. We'd be forgiven for thinking that this doesn't add up.

This is where faith and hope are of such significance. Having faith and positive belief in the face of difficulty is sometimes called 'spiritual bypassing'. When I first encountered this term, I felt conflicted about the notion that something of paramount importance to me could be passed off as what sounded like a crutch or a coping mechanism. However, I soon reminded myself that if hope, faith and belief are not rooted in the concept or person you're cultivating spiritual practices around, then yes, they will fall short. What's crucial here is faith and who or what it's founded on.

This chapter's 'Faith focus' will look at faith and hope in Jesus and its significance through the real and lived experience of King David, who, in one of the many psalms he wrote, confidently said, 'I believe that I shall look upon the goodness of the Lord in the land of the living!' (Psalm 27:13, ESV), while his enemies lay in wait for him. We'll explore what having confident hope and faith can look like in the midst of less-than-hopeful circumstances. We'll also take a glance at Mark 9 for a simple prayer we can echo when hope and faith feel far off, but we know we need them.

Why hope?

In a world where wellbeing can take on different forms, hope offers an underpinning. Many business gurus will say that 'hope isn't a strategy'. They stand in good company. Benjamin Franklin is quoted as saying that 'he who lives upon hope will die fasting'. My belief is that while hope may not be a strategy, it is a standpoint. It is a declaration of sorts and a line in the sand which affords the person who dares to hold on to it a freedom which other areas of wellbeing don't necessarily provide. Hope suggests a holding on *in spite of* circumstances, a willingness to keep trying – even if the trying is simply believing that things can be better than they currently are.

This disposition is vital. Not only does it ground the one who carries it, but it sends a clear message to those who want that carrier to give up and submit to hopelessness. The hopeful disposition digs its heels in and tells everyone who gets within sniffing distance of it that it's not going to be moved. It's safe to say that hope had taken hold of the apostle Paul when he said in Philippians 4:11: 'I am not saying this because I am in need, for I have learned to be content whatever the circumstances.' We don't need to go too far into what's documented of Paul's life to recognise that it was far from plain sailing. His anchor was Jesus, and perhaps hope gave him the strength to lower it.

The truth is, hope doesn't always get the best press. Those who are hopeful have sometimes been viewed as 'head in the clouds' types who don't have a firm grasp on reality. This, however, couldn't be further from the truth. Many psychologists now believe that hope is a key component in truly understanding human flourishing. From a faith perspective, scholars and thinkers in the church have been studying hope for centuries. For example, Thomas Aquinas, one of the greatest theologians of the medieval period, defined hope as 'a theological virtue by which man, relying on God's strength, seeks an arduous but possible good'. Here, hope is outlined as both the endpoint (the virtue) and the means or journey to go about obtaining it. Beyond theologians, however, hope is also heralded among philosophers and psychologists alike.

Thinking hope

The link between science and hope may not seem obvious. However, the more we learn about hope, the more it will confirm to us that we can do a whole lot more with it than we can without it. And hope is important not only for our doing, but also for our being. *The Oxford Handbook of Hope* states: 'Hope is positively related to experiences of positive emotion and psychological health and inversely associated with experiences of negative emotion and psycho-pathology.'[2] While objects of hope may differ, based on a number of aspects such as worldview, there is a central thought among scholars that, at least at its basic foundation of 'positive expectations for the future', hope is significant.

It is also rarely, if ever, dangerous or harmful. In fact, more often than not, even in excruciating circumstances, it is quite the opposite. There is an increasing body of research and work which demonstrates the benefits of hope not only on our wellbeing, but also on our overall mental health, not to mention our academic and physical achievements.

There is, however, an element of our own agency that comes into play when it comes to hope benefiting our wellbeing and beyond. As clichéd as the 'glass half empty or glass half full' analogy is, there is something significant about it. People referred to in certain texts as 'high-hope individuals' maintain a positive disposition towards their goals, focusing on the possibilities of success as opposed to the alternative possibility of failure as they approach them. The good news here is that these high-hope individuals haven't simply lucked out with this disposition, but rather they harness agency in the pursuit of their goals; for example, by more readily asking for help or drawing on alternative resources. These are habits and traits which can be developed and then go on to cultivate more hope, further indicating that hope is a renewable resource. Viewing hope as a renewable resource also offers the opportunity to collectively draw upon one another. When one individual might be lacking hope, a friend, colleague or family member is likely to be able to offer a more hopeful perspective that they're better able to see at that point.

Faith focus: 'I believe. Help my unbelief.'

The Bible is filled with stories of people and places who faced such extreme hardship that it doesn't bear thinking about. This is, of course, not dissimilar to the difficulty and devastation which so many across the globe face today. So you'd be forgiven for thinking that a focus on hope is either tone deaf or distasteful. However, history is not void of it. In fact, history is so hope-filled it should give us more pause for thought and reflection than it often does.

King David is one of these historical figures who held on to hope in the midst of danger. At the time of writing Psalm 27, it is believed that David was in hiding while his enemies were lying in wait for him. The opening of the psalm is a profession of hope despite the bleak backdrop. Verse 1 is a clear declaration of who God is to David. His reminder to himself that God is Lord of his life (and indeed of all life) gives him the confidence to utter two rhetorical questions, which are undoubtedly hope-filled: 'Whom shall I fear?' and 'Of whom shall I be afraid?' Verses 2–3 highlight these circumstances, and this is significant. Hope doesn't dismiss reality and put a plaster of toxic positivity over something which needs addressing. Rather, it puts those circumstances into perspective and, in this case, does so in light of who God is in the midst of them.

After giving himself some reassurance and reminders of God's promises in verses 4–6, the psalm changes structure and becomes a direct prayer to God. David cries out for help and makes pleas to God from verses 7 to 12. He does this despite the opening four verses providing such certainty on his standpoint of who God is to him.

This, I believe, is of importance for believers today. Hope isn't passive. Hope isn't simply an acknowledgement of who God is while we wait for him to prove us right. Rather, it's an active stance. That act could simply be an acknowledgement and a belief, or it could be movement and action in the direction of what we're hopeful for. We're told in the book of James that 'faith without deeds is dead' and that faith is actually made complete in action (James 2:20–26). This is why David doesn't simply make declarations of who God is, but instead goes on to cry out to the one he knows has the power and authority to change his circumstances.

The last two verses of Psalm 27 see David reminding and encouraging himself once again. The final verse (v. 14) serves as a reminder for us, just as it was for David – a reminder to wait. Hope waits. Once we've cried out and done all that we can from our own very human and frail position, we remind ourselves that God's timeline does not look the same as ours. We wait for him to act from a disposition of hope and faith that he is who he says he is and who we believe him to be.

At this point I'd like us to explore a simple, authentic and hope-filled prayer which we can echo when hope is all we have, while simultane- ously it feels hard to hold on to. In Mark 9, we read of the disciples being caught in a dispute with a large crowd of people. When Jesus eventually reaches them and enquires what's been going on, a father in the crowd shares that he'd brought his demon-possessed son to the disciples in the hope that they would be able to cast the demon out. They weren't, and now there appears to be a debate going on as to why. In verse 20, the boy is brought to Jesus and as a result of being in his presence, falls to the ground, foaming at the mouth. Jesus asks how long this has been happening and the father confirms it has been the case since childhood. At the end of verse 22, the father, clearly in the depths of desperation, says, 'But if you can do anything, have compassion on us and help us' (ESV). Verses 23–24 read:

> '"If you can"?' said Jesus. 'Everything is possible for one who believes.' Immediately the boy's father exclaimed, 'I do believe; help me overcome my unbelief!'

It's that prayer of doubt-tinged hope and faith which I so resonate with and believe to be important for each of us.

Just like hope, faith is messy and imperfect. What this sorrow-filled father knew is what many of us know to be true of ourselves. Yes, there is a foundation and root of belief. However, just as present, albeit sometimes louder or quieter, is a doubt, which we feel guilty and uncertain about. The desperate words of this father – 'I believe. Help my unbelief' – remind us that faith and hope in God aren't about being perfect, about holding on to them with such certainty that being rocked is somehow evidence that they've disappeared. What it can indicate instead is that we're humans with a very real spectrum of emotions.

What should encourage us even further, however, is Jesus' response. He healed the boy completely. This hope-filled and yet somehow half-hearted prayer of the boy's father led to the healing of his son. What might hope lead us to believe and, in turn, act upon as we utter similar words to our heavenly Father?

Food for thought

1 What disposition do you currently hold when it comes to hope? Has any of what's been shared in this chapter caused you to think differently? If so, what actions might it cause you to take?

2 How has hope previously arisen for you in the face of challenging past circumstances, and how might this serve as a reference for how you might handle current or future challenges?

3 Have you ever had that sneaking suspicion that hope has to be whole in order for it to be real? What can even the glimmers of hope you hold right now cause you to dream and do about your future?

3

Wellbeing and our mindset

It was 2017 and I'd recently started my own online business. The fact I was no longer a classroom teacher after years of that being my only career was simultaneously exhilarating and overwhelming. Being in charge of my own time and the way in which I worked had been a steep learning curve, but one which I embraced with both hands. However, I had to finally acknowledge that what had got me *here* (my first few clients and the ability to work full time on my business) wouldn't get me *there* (replacing and surpassing my previous salary and my digital courses being filled) hit me hard. I knew it was time to find some support.

Having had a coach when I first started my business, I knew the power of coaching and therefore knew it was time to start working with one again. When I did, though, I wasn't aware of the journey we'd take together as I took the next step in growing my business.

'I've done everything': I remember the complaint I made as we started our call that morning. I was frustrated and overwhelmed at the amount of work I'd been doing for seemingly so few results. That's the part which no one tells you about starting your own business. Yes, you're the creative force doing the work you love (in my case, writing and teaching), but you're also the advertiser, the marketer, the sales person, the graphic designer and the account manager, to name just a few roles you take on when embarking on this labour of love. I carried on: 'I've been posting daily for ages, I've been reaching out to previous clients and I've been messaging anyone who's even sniffed in the direction of my offer. Despite doing everything, I've got nothing.'

My coach paused, seemingly nonplussed by my outpouring of upset at the current situation. 'What sort of emotion are you bringing to these interactions?' she asked. This question was followed up with: 'How are you actually feeling right now?' Despite wanting to leap through the screen, screaming in frustration, I decided to pause and think about what it was she was asking me. The truth is, the emotion I was bringing to those interactions was the same as the emotion I was bringing to this call. Frustrated and, in some ways, already expecting the worst before even giving the opportunity a chance. What my coach was getting at was the fact that, although my actions were seemingly the done thing in this instance, I'd not given a second of attention to my mindset or emotional state during these interactions.

Maintaining a positive mindset is about far more than feel-good vibes and painting on a smile when you feel anything other than positive. A positive mindset is about looking at options and sensing peace before acting accordingly.

Digging deeper

The Bible talks about mindset, both directly and indirectly, more than we might initially realise. When we think about the story of Hannah in 1 Samuel, for example, we see a woman grieving the fact she has no child. To take it one step further, we actually note in 1 Samuel 1:5 that God had 'closed her womb'. This didn't stop Hannah crying out to the Lord in her grief and desperation. At one point, Eli, the priest of the temple, Hannah visited year upon year, believed Hannah to be drunk. The way in which she was pouring her heart out before the Lord was so real and vulnerable that he could draw no other conclusion. The truth, however, was very different. Hannah's husband even makes an inquiry at one point, wondering why she's so upset and asking whether he's not worth more to her than ten sons (v. 8). The emotion and grief Hannah felt was clearly apparent to those around her. In verse 17, Eli says to Hannah, 'Go in peace, and may the God of Israel grant you what you have asked of him.' What is most striking, however, is Hannah's response: 'She said, "May your servant find favour in your eyes." Then she went her way and ate something, and her face was no longer downcast' (v. 18).

I don't believe that after years of grief, desperation and sadness, Hannah simply no longer felt sad about the fact she didn't have a child. In fact, I'm sure that she did. Rather, I think that she made a *decision* to shift her attitude and her mindset and begin to believe that what Eli had prayed over her in the previous verse would be true – that she would indeed have peace and be granted what she had been asking for. We find, in verse 20, that God did indeed answer her prayers when Samuel bursts on to the scene.

Hannah did not simply decide to 'fake it till she made it'; nor, during her wait, did she simply stop feeling any of that anguish she'd felt previously. Rather her faith-filled disposition caused her to think differently about her circumstances and, in turn, she was able to act differently as a result. Again, here we see source outweighing circumstances, but those circumstances being in no way demeaned or downplayed.

In this chapter's 'Faith focus', we'll be looking at passages within the letter to the Philippians, which was written as a form of encouragement to the Philippian church to continue persevering in the faith as they served God and each other. This might sound simple, but the reality was far from it. Philippians helps us unpack how we might live with the inconsistencies and inconveniences of everyday life while simultaneously operating from a faith-filled and Christ-focused perspective.

Fixed vs growth mindset

When my son was learning to dress himself, he'd often get frustrated. He'd put one leg into his tracksuit bottoms only to turn the other trouser leg inside out or end up with both legs in one hole. In these instances, he'd often want us to do it for him, or he would end up saying things like, 'I'm never going to be able to do this.' At that point we decided to introduce the concept of the fixed and growth mindset to him. Not only did we introduce it to him, he chose to take it on and, during those previously frustrating moments, instead of him declaring what he wasn't able to do, we'd sometimes find him saying things like, 'I can do this. Growth mindset!' The circumstances hadn't changed (it was still hard for him to get himself dressed), but his attitude towards the circumstances had changed from what he deemed to be difficult to what he recognised as doable.

Before looking at growth and fixed, let's explore what is meant by a mindset. Beyond simply thinking about positive and negative, Alia Crum, Peter Salovey and Shawn Achor define a mindset as 'a mental frame or lens that selectively organises and encodes information'.[3] The way in which we organise this information is largely based on our experiences as we move through the world.

The psychologist Carol Dweck, who essentially discovered growth and fixed mindsets through her research, explores what each of these dispositions look like in practice.

Someone with a fixed mindset will believe that their current abilities, attitude, talent and even intelligence are fixed traits they have. Because of this, they'll be less likely to try something new for fear that it will reveal their potential limitations or inadequacies. People with this type of mindset are typically more prone to giving up or potentially not putting as much effort into a task as others might. This behaviour stems from the belief that if the traits which they possess come naturally to them and are largely fixed, exhaustive effort will bear little fruit.

An individual operating within a growth mindset, on the other hand, understands that the skillset and characteristics they possess are not fixed; their abilities can be enhanced through hard work and effort. A person with a growth mindset won't avoid challenges, but will rather see them as significant opportunities for learning and growth. They tend to more readily persevere in difficult situations.

Dweck's work suggests that those who adopt a growth mindset are generally more likely to achieve what they set out to do. Their resilience and ability to persevere in the face of difficulty cause them to have a more rounded and robust outlook on life and its challenges. In fact, some of her research explores how praise of a child for intelligence can undermine a child's performance in a particular endeavour. What's proven to be more effective is praise for effort. Children who receive praise for their intelligence typically find themselves choosing activities that continue to prove their intelligence. This means they tend to pick easier challenges or things they're already good at, as opposed to children who have been praised for effort, who will continue to challenge themselves, knowing that the effort itself is praiseworthy as opposed to just the results of it.

Thankfully, a growth mindset can be nurtured in anybody willing to adapt some of their ways of thinking, due to the God-given gift of neuroplasticity. Early thinkers suggested that the brain is fixed in both its function and its structure. It's now widely accepted that in fact the brain has strong capabilities to change and form new neural pathways and connections. This phenomenon is termed neuroplasticity: that the brain can indeed change through reorganisation and growth. This is why the notion of fixed and growth mindsets isn't just a school of thought we choose to subscribe to or not, but rather an affirmation of the way in which our brains have been designed from the very beginning. We just have to decide whether to exercise our minds to such a degree that it will have a bearing on our lives.

Given this fact, those of us with a worldview and outlook rooted in faith have even more liberty to operate within a growth mindset. Believing in the creator God of the Bible automatically leads us to believe in the goodness and truth of what he's created. It can be a lot easier to notice God's goodness in the created world when we look at nature, for example. A walk through the rolling hills on an autumnal morning as we take in the crisp air and the myriad of colours on the trees probably gives us little reason to doubt the presence of a creator who designed the scene before us.

However, when we, with our negative tendencies, both in our outward actions and attitudes and in our thought-lives, are asked to consider whether the mindset we possess is God-given too, we might pause for thought. We theoretically know we've been made in God's image. But when our thoughts run wild and our actions sometimes follow them, we'd be forgiven for doubting that something so seemingly fickle and changeable could adapt and take on significant growth for the better.

Faith focus: Yours in Christ Jesus

The book of Philippians is full of encouragement to the church at Philippi to *think,* and therefore *do,* differently. This church was significant for the author Paul, because it was the first he planted in Europe. His compassion and heart for these believers is evident throughout this epistle. What is striking, though, is the attention Paul gives not to continuing because they're believers and they know that God has instructed them to, but rather because of who Christ is *in* them.

It is for this very reason that our ability to operate within a growth mindset as believers is far more possible than we might initially consider when only looking at our own abilities and immediate options.

Towards the end of Philippians, Paul says: 'Finally, brothers and sisters, whatever is true, whatever is noble, whatever is right, whatever is pure, whatever is lovely, whatever is admirable – if anything is excellent or praiseworthy – think about such things' (Philippians 4:8). In the first instance, we might believe this to be a charge from the apostle to block out anything negative and remain fixated only on the good. It certainly gives that impression when it's posted across social media as a motivational quote. While it is a deeply powerful verse just read on its own, reading it in the context of the rest of the book allows us to grasp a deeper understanding of what Paul is getting at here, much of which seems to come down to the mindset and disposition these believers should be adopting and indeed taking advantage of.

In Philippians 2:4 Paul talks about humility and unpacks the notion that believers need to be looking not just at their own needs but also the needs of those around them. They are to have the interests of their fellow brothers and sisters at the forefront of their minds and actions. He goes on in verse 5 to say that having this mindset isn't something to strive for, because they don't need to; it's actually already theirs in Christ Jesus. The beauty of this is that it is also already ours too. What was readily available to the church at Philippi – the Holy Spirit – is also within us who believe. The example which Paul goes on to use here is Jesus himself. Paul unpacks Jesus' very nature and his utter humanness in verses 6–8. Jesus knew what it was like to be a human being with needs and wants and was yet able to bring these under submission before his Father. This wasn't just physical submission, but mental. This ability was supernatural, and it's an ability we have too. Just as it was for the Philippians, it's ours too in Christ.

In Philippians 3, Paul talks to the church about what it means to keep going, to continue to persevere no matter what. Like all humans, their lived experiences were far from perfect, and at times, they would look to each other for someone to blame. Paul encourages them to keep the faith – to continue in what they've been taught despite their differences and the apparent ease they might have in falling back into practices they adopted before they knew Christ. In verse 15, Paul says: 'All of us, then, who are mature should take such a view of things. And if on some point you think differently, that too God will make clear to you.' This phrase 'taking such a view of things', or 'think this way', is taken from the Greek root word *phroneō*. This word can be literally taken to mean 'to exercise the mind'. Even the early church back in approximately AD62 had the option to adopt Christ-filled mindset practices, which would cause them to stop strife and also stand firm in the gospel-hope entrusted to them. This is certainly something which has stood the test of time and would also be of benefit to us in today's church.

This word *phroneō* is only found 29 times in the New Testament and eight of these instances fall within the book of Philippians. What can we learn from the apostle Paul's emphasis on this adapted mindset? Here was a growing church with lots of exciting things going for them, but which was also prone to forget to live out their calling as citizens of heaven, being easily tempted to look to the ways of the world to obtain what they wanted. It doesn't sound too dissimilar to today, does it? Paul's constant reminder of this new way of thinking the church of Philippi could adopt in everything from individual squabbles (see Philippians 4:2) to a way of operating in all things throughout their lives on earth (see Philippians 2:2) is also something we can run with. Like the Philippians, though, we don't do this in and of our own strength, but rather because of who Jesus is in us by the power of the Holy Spirit. We have the privilege of calling on him and enquiring after him to change our hearts and our minds by his power so that we might live the full and flourishing lives he has for us.

Food for thought

1 What would you say your 'mind maintenance' practice currently looks like? Are you willing to see and therefore do things differently when it comes to the way in which you think?

2 Do you find ourself largely operating with a fixed mindset or a growth mindset? Why? If you haven't already, are you willing to further explore the benefits of a growth mindset?

3 As a Christian, how much have you taken responsibility for shaping your mind and bringing your mindset into submission under Christ? How has this action (or lack of action) impacted you?

4

Wellbeing and the TIME framework: an introduction

My introduction to teaching was an interesting one, to say the least. I was 22, just out of university and eager and excited to embark on my new career. I had chosen to enter teaching through the Graduate Teacher Programme, which meant that my learning was done 'on the job' through school placements, with a day or two every couple of weeks spent in lectures at university. My first placement was in what OFSTED had recognised as a failing school. As I walked into the drama studio for the first time, I was greeted by a 15-year-old girl who was taller than me. 'Are you our new drama teacher?' she sniffed. 'We made our last one cry.' Needless to say, this wasn't quite the 'I'm going to change the world' type of first day I'd expected. Further down the line, though, that class became a firm favourite of mine and I don't recall them driving me to tears once (not that class, anyway).

With over 75% of people aged 16–64 in employment, many of whom work at least 40 hours a week, there's no getting away from the significance of work in many of our lives. It should go without saying, then, that we should pay attention to how we're working and why we're working, while reflecting on whether the current way in which we're doing it is contributing to our wellbeing or lack thereof.

While it's dangerous to place the entirety of our identity and worth in our achievements and accolades, many of us understandably form a sense of affiliation and affinity with what we spend so much of our time doing.

The reason I developed my TIME framework and created The Time Journal® was because when I had my first child, I found myself delighted and overjoyed in so many ways, while simultaneously feeling lost in so many others. After my seven-year career as a teacher, I worked for our church for a time and then moved on to run my own business as a course creator and coach. Over a decade of my life had been given to hard work and carving out my career path, which I loved. Consciously or not, I'd certainly formed some parts of myself at work. Whether from the feedback I received (both positive and negative), which had shaped me, the hours I'd put in mastering my craft, or the muscle memory I'd developed doing something which resulted in a particular outcome so many times – without it, I felt adrift.

Another child later, I know now that this feeling isn't uncommon for new parents or for those whose lives have been shaped by other significant experiences. I also know that, looking after children, I was – and indeed am – still working, but just in a different way. That said, I was proud of the person I'd spent so much time becoming, and I didn't want to lose her in the midst of the rest of my life. I wanted an expression of my ambition and my goals in the midst of my caregiving responsibilities. I didn't want motherhood to mean that I could no longer dream big about my work, and I didn't want my work to be so all-consuming that it meant the only way I could get anything done was by being so laser-focused that nothing else got the best of me.

Speaking to a number of my mum friends, I wasn't alone in this sentiment, which is why I was determined to create something which allowed for work to be looked at through a wellbeing lens. I no longer had the capacity nor the desire to sit at my laptop from morning till evening (and into the early hours sometimes) with all of my attention focused on the task at hand. But it was certainly important to me and countless others that we still worked outside of our caregiving responsibilities. That's when the Time & Pace® framework was born.

Digging deeper

It can be easy to place all our identity into our output. I'm sure I'm not the only one who has been guilty of this. There are so many helpful personality tests out there which strengthen our connection to an aspect of our character and in some ways can mark who we are. While these tests are useful, placing the entirety of our identity into being an 'achiever' or a 'pioneer', for example (both outcomes I've received in taking different personality tests), can be entirely detrimental.

As Christians, we don't have to be tempted by this way of thinking. Rather, we can take hold of and remind ourselves that God cares for us as a whole individual; one who will experience both joy and despair, who will have seasons of more visible achievement and seasons where no one will know who we are, what we've done and our output is behind closed doors. God sees it all, knows about it all and cares about it all.

Psalm 139 beautifully illustrates this truth that God is concerned with every aspect of us. In my days as a teacher, I shared the fact I was a Christian with my class at the time. It just so happened that, because this class was a group of students I'd been asked to educate off-site as part of the school's alternative provision, I was teaching them in a church building the school had hired out. One day, during breaktime, one of the students picked up a Bible and started flicking through it. One of my friends who happened to be in the church at the time, as they worked there, shouted over to my student, 'Check out Psalm

139.' I helped her to find it, and then she sat in silence for a while as she read the words. She commented on how 'inspirational' and 'motivating' she found the text to be. Then it was time for lessons again, and I didn't think much more of it. It wasn't until the next day, when she handed me a tea-stained piece of A4 paper with the words of Psalm 139 etched over it that I realised the significance of what she had read the day before. She told me she'd really enjoyed reading it and that she thought I might like what she'd written. She was right. In fact, I later framed that piece of paper as a reminder that God can speak to anyone at any point and make a significant impact.

Psalm 139 sees the psalmist recognise the truth that God will never leave them – not even if they were to settle on the far side of the sea (v. 9) nor if they were to hide themselves in darkness (v. 11). Verse 14 says: 'I praise you because I am fearfully and wonderfully made; your works are wonderful, I know that full well.' What I love about this outburst of praise is that the psalmist is admiring who God is in them and who they're created to be. This too is the cry of our hearts as we praise him for who he's made us to be – all of who he's made us to be. Our 'Faith focus' in this chapter will visit Paul in Athens in Acts 17 as he explores what it means for God to have access to all areas of our life.

Progress without pressure

In our increasingly fast-paced world, it can be easy to get swept up in the urgency which everything seems to have attached to it. 'Act now', 'Buy today before time runs out' and 'Do this before it's too late' are all messages we've no doubt grown accustomed to hearing as we go about our day-to-day lives. This way of thinking has also seeped into the personal development world with notions such as 'Nice guys finish last'. While I appreciate the fact that hard work does often yield positive results, the idea that this has to be done to the detriment of our mental health and wellbeing is where these messages fall short.

Don't get me wrong, these brands and businesses won't say: 'Do this and damage your emotional, mental and physical health in the process.' But they might say: 'With all of the calories and nutrients you need packed into this one bottle, you can drink this on the go.' On the surface, this sounds like a great message: we don't have to stop for lunch and we still get all of the nutrients, vitamins and calories we need from this one bottle. But what does it encourage us to do instead? Keep going, keep pushing, keep working.

We're human beings, not human doings. And yet modern-day hacks like these don't cause us to think about where we could do with being more present or where we could afford to take more pause. Instead they encourage us to think about whether it's possible to press on that bit further and to take a bit more out of our already stretched margins. The problem with this is that if everyone's doing it and we're caught in this trap of needing to perform and be constantly at the peak of our game, or at least always 'on', none of us do very well at encouraging each other to go and grow at a pace which is relevant for our life stage. It seems obvious, but life is not one size fits all. The idea that we should all be doing the exact same amount in all areas of our life, no matter what we've got going on, feels absurd, and yet, it's the unsaid expectation.

When I launched The Time Journal®, which houses my framework, I was relieved when people started sharing testimonials with me about how it supported them in focusing on their day with more intention, ease and clarity and, rather than it being a tool for 'maximising the day', it had given them more room for pause. This is what the professional and personal development world can miss sometimes – the fact that we're hardwired for rest and recreation just as much as we are for work. What can be especially toxic about the sort of mindset which suggests that we're a type of robot who can just keep going without any form of recharge, is that it can all too easily root our worth and our overall value in our output and productivity levels.

We'll address this notion in more depth later, but it's important to note that this is why I believe our current understanding of work–life balance isn't one which makes sense.

There are and absolutely will be times during which we are more productive and driven towards our goals. Equally, there are times when life's circumstances cause us to rethink our priorities and we can even be forced to stop. If our worth is based on our output alone, what do these moments suggest about who we are?

What if maximising the day took on a totally different meaning? What if it really was to think through where you needed to be *present* first? This can be tricky to navigate. If we only worked when we felt like it, we wouldn't be the most reliable for those depending on us. However, being reliable and completely ignoring our own needs and intuition are two different things.

> 'If X didn't bring the hustle out of you,
> it's not in you.'

This is a quote which did a number of rounds, in particular during the global pandemic, with the 'X' being the year 2020. At first glance, I wholeheartedly agreed. If an especially challenging season, where you've been forced to be housebound or you've come to a point where you'll do whatever it takes to make ends meet, doesn't cause you to work as if your life depends on it, what will? But then, I'm glad to say, I came to my senses.

This quote is problematic in a number of ways, but let's start with what I think is the most important criticism. It perpetuates the notion that we live to work and that if we suddenly amass time which hasn't previously been accounted for in our calendars, we should use it to hustle, to be more productive, to work harder.

I don't think I'll ever tire of reiterating the fact that we're human beings and not human doings. So if you do, by God's grace, unexpectedly get a bit more time back, that should never be something which guilt-trips you into what you 'should' be doing with that time.

It's similar to the well-intentioned suggestions people have when you're on maternity leave to 'sleep when the baby sleeps', for example, as though this is the only option you have during nap times and that anything else you'd like to accomplish or get on top of isn't the done thing, especially when you're complaining about sleepless nights. Again, shed the should. You are not required to do what other people would do in your circumstances. It's absolutely fine, and in fact, important, to lean in and listen to where and how you're being led.

The Time & Pace® framework is definitely about supporting you in being productive, but it first asks the question about where you need to be present. This means that your public performance isn't the benchmark of your success at any given moment. It's important to note the *public* aspect to this too. Sometimes you're doing the deep work behind the scenes, which no one sees, perhaps even work which is laying the foundation for your future.

But foundations aren't often met with fanfares, are they? Let's get used to being okay with that. Let's get used to enjoying going deep in the dark room of development, even if we don't have anything outward to show for it in the first instance. Performance-based metrics don't mean much unless they're supported by action which will allow for this so-called success to be sustainable.

Here are some alternative endings to the initial quote I shared, which you can try on for size if you're allowing yourself the option and grace to take up space in a way which makes sense for you and your current season right now, as opposed to hurtling towards a pressurised productivity goal: 'If X didn't bring the hustle out of you…'

1 You were putting your energy into coping and you're much better now for not spreading your already thinly spread self even thinner.
2 You were healing and recharging.
3 You were spending more time with your family.
4 You were sacrificing your goals in the short-term, in order to place the priority on something more significant long-term.
5 You were resting.
6 You were taking stock and reevaluating what you want your life to look like and whether what you're currently doing is a true reflection of this.

Faith focus: 'In him, we live and move and have our being'

> The God who made the world and everything in it is the Lord of heaven and earth and does not live in temples built by human hands. And he is not served by human hands, as if he needed anything. Rather, he himself gives everyone life and breath and everything else.
> ACTS 17:24–25

In above passage, the apostle Paul is speaking to the Areopagus, a group of men with authority over both the civil and the religious goings-on in Athens. Their authority and status didn't faze Paul as he recognised that he answered to a much higher authority. In the verse prior to this one, he goes as far as to make an example of them by pointing out that one of the gods they worship is described as 'unknown'.

These were men who were used to gods that represented certain areas of their lives: 'fertility' (Artemis), 'victory' (Nike) and 'wealth' (Plutus) to name a few. For Paul, to suggest that the one true God would be boxed in alongside all of these other gods wasn't acceptable. Imagine for a moment a rolling landscape complete with evergreen trees, snow-capped mountains and winding, gravel paths for as far as the eye can see. And then picture in the corner of this scene a tiny red brick house. Imagine someone designing this beautiful, picturesque landscape, only for someone else to come along and tell them they could only enjoy it by sitting in the little red brick house and looking out of the window.

This, of course, wouldn't make sense. If someone has created and designed something, they typically have total rights to do with it as they please. Have we made our God too small? Have we given him a window seat and said that we do appreciate him watching over us, ensuring our safety and perhaps seeing to it that we have a decent job, but we don't understand how he could be involved in everything. Perhaps it's not even something we want, if we were to be totally honest. Maybe we like the idea of him sitting in the little red brick house while we get on with our lives. We know where to find him if things get really messy, after all.

The truth, however, is that our God is limitless. He who was before anything else cannot be contained or confined to something we've made for him or to just one area of our lives. He wants the 'access all areas' pass and doesn't need to wait for permission to be granted, although he does occasionally humour us by waiting for an invite.

This is what Paul was getting at with the Areopagus. God is the God of the universe and not of some area which suited them. He even refers to the Cretan philosopher Epimenides, who says of God: 'In him we live and move and have our being' (v. 28). It can be so easy to place ourselves on Paul's side in this instance, arguing that of course we want God involved in all we do. But how easy it is to find ourselves on the side of the Areopagus, spending our days listening out for the most profound wisdom (or the best productivity tips and tricks) without fully and tangibly recognising that God wants access to *all* areas. Our working, our resting and everything in between should bring God into the centre of it all.

To close this chapter and to circle back to our source being more significant than our circumstances when it comes to wellbeing, it's important to note here that I am not only referring to our source being more significant when times are tough because of the firm foundation our faith provides in our ability to get up again when we've been knocked down. I'm also talking about it being of more importance even when our circumstances are the best they've ever been. If we take our enjoyment of the current goodness we've been blessed with and begin to place whole parts of our identity and trust there, what do we do when those things give way? God doesn't talk about the 'access all areas' idea from a place of manipulation and control but rather from a place of love. He knows he's the only person, circumstance or thing which won't fail and so he urges us to turn to him in both the bad *and* the good times as we remind ourselves of where our stability is.

Food for thought

1 Are you currently giving the same energy to rest and recreation that you are to work and productivity?

2 What aspect of your life are you currently being called to lay the foundations for – even if the results won't be recognised instantly? What or who can hold you accountable to making this happen (without the fanfare)?

3 How does the fact that God wants access to *all* areas make you feel? Have you found yourself more typically only inviting him into certain areas?

5

Wellbeing and our goals (E)

The French writer Antoine de Saint-Exupéry (1900–44) said: 'A goal without a plan is just a wish.' I'm sure I'm not the only one who can attest to the truth in these words. I was the girl in secondary school who aimed to do well with revision when it came to GCSE exams. I bought the highlighters and the relevant text books. My little desk in my bedroom looked pristine with its sections for everything. I'm sure I even created a revision timetable at some point – largely influenced by the fact that it meant I got to use my new highlighters. The truth, though, is that in spite of my good intentions, my revision was still relatively lacklustre and certainly didn't follow the pattern of my shiny timetable.

Fast forward to 2013, the year I got married. I had a goal to tone up for my wedding day. Vain, yes, but I knew the type of dress I wanted and what I wanted to look like in it. So I made a plan, not dissimilar to the revision timetable of teenage me a decade or so prior. I planned what I was going to eat for the next few months and noted when I was going to go to the gym. It so happened that the time which worked best was early morning with a friend of mine and so 6.00 am workouts became the norm for a while. In short, with a lot of discipline and hard work, I achieved my goal by the time my wedding day rolled around.

When it came to starting my first online business in 2016, my goal was to go full-time by a particular date. My role as a teacher had been made redundant, but by God's grace I'd been offered a part-time role working for our church. I eagerly embraced that job and worked hard while simultaneously being quite surprised at the doors God seemed to be opening with the little online course I'd created. It was called 'Chosen: a mindset journey to walking in your worth' and was for Christian women who wanted to better understand themselves through God's loving lens. Having started a basic blog in 2011 (before blogs were even the done thing), I was stopped in my tracks at the realisation that this work I was doing in the online world was first, being paid attention to by anyone outside my family and close friends and, second, could indeed be remunerated. I resolved to really make a go of it and start marketing my other services and products online. Within a matter of months I was able to go full-time, still operating as an active volunteer at church but having autonomy over my time and energy as a small business owner. And the rest is history.

This chapter will explore some of the nuanced differences with regard to what leads to meeting and surpassing some goals while falling short of others.

Digging deeper

Because of the bad press which goal-setting can sometimes get, with those against it putting it in the 'hustle culture' bracket of work, it can be easy to turn a blind eye to it. As Christians, however, there's a further reason why we can disregard it. All too commonly in faith-based circles, the notion of purpose and goals can be met with the answer that our goal is to 'make disciples' and of course to 'glorify God'. While these things are true, they aren't mutually exclusive to having goals for how we'll use the gifts and calling God has so graciously granted us.

I'm always struck by the specific details provided for in the building of the tabernacle, which is outlined in Exodus. The beauty, the craftsmanship and the fact that not one single aspect is overlooked should give us pause for thought if we're still questioning the value of having concrete plans for our life and our work. Although the context here is very different, I hope it'll encourage you in considering whether or not God is invested in the finer details. Exodus 25—28 give instructions ranging from the length of the curtains down to what the priests should wear. In fact, in 28:3, it reads: 'You shall speak to all the skillful, whom I have filled with a spirit of skill, that they may make Aaron's garments to consecrate him for my priesthood' (ESV). Imagine this command for *all* the skillful people (who God blessed with those skills in the first place) to work on the clothes which just one man will wear. God is a God of the details. Yes, he has and does go before us, and leads and guides our steps as we walk in accordance with his Spirit. But he also grants us particular abilities and asks that we put them to use.

Although scholars' understanding of the authorship of the book of Proverbs isn't totally conclusive, it's widely believed that Solomon wrote most of it. Solomon was renowned for his wisdom, and he wrote a book that we still have access to today. That to me is reason enough to pay attention to it. Proverbs is filled with God's wisdom pertaining to a number of aspects of our lives, such as how we treat one another, how we steward our money and, indeed, how we work. In this chapter, we'll explore some of this wisdom by looking at verses in chapters 16 and 19, as well as taking a brief look at Colossians 3:23–24.

Starting with the end in mind

'Start with the end in the mind' is a familiar expression, but is it worthwhile advice?

How much of our time is spent in reaction mode, as opposed to taking small steps towards a goal we've already mapped out? Even more than this – have we spent so much time in reaction mode that we've not even given ourselves the opportunity to think about the goals we want to achieve?

Of course, we will at various points need to respond to people urgently, for example, to drop what we're doing in order to go and pick up a poorly child. There are circumstances which we inevitably cannot plan for. However, if the majority of our time is spent reacting to 'emergencies' (either yours or other people's), then those goals you've had in mind for what you want to do with your life will be a lot harder to reach. And they'll be even harder to reach if you've never even given them any thought because of how busy you are with everything else.

Literally defined, according to the Oxford English Dictionary, the word 'expectation' is 'the belief that something will happen or be the case'. From my experience, belief in something happening is quite often enhanced when I know that I've done all I'm able to do in order to help the process along. The rest isn't up to me. I don't think we're meant to sit with a strong belief that something will happen but be unwilling to do anything to play our part in moving closer to that goal.

This is why the fourth and final pillar of the TIME framework, which is related to our goals, is 'expectation'. When we truly set our minds to something, we tend to find a way to make it happen – by hook or by crook. It's not always perfect, but more often than not, it's done.

However, I'm interested in expectations being a lot more connected with our normal day-to-day lives, as opposed to the 'otherworldly' or 'one day' type category we might otherwise put them into. So with that, a question:

 What is one thing you hope to achieve in the next 90 days?

Your answer might be something work related, health related, family related, or anything in between. The point is, it's something you know that you want to make happen in the next three months or less.

Now, think about the things on your to-do list for today or for the next week if you've mapped out that far. Do your daily actions correlate with the one thing you hope to achieve in the next 90 days? If not, why not?

This is, of course, an ambiguous question. The reasons for today's actions not looking like your overall expectations and hopes could be manifold. So, for a moment, let's tune into the belief part of the definition of expectation.

In his book *The Long View*, Matthew Kelly writes: 'Most people overestimate what they can do in a day, and underestimate what they can do in a month. We overestimate what we can do in a year, and underestimate what we can accomplish in a decade.'[4] With that in mind, when I asked what you wanted to achieve in the next 90 days, did you roll your eyes at how little time that sounded? Did you internally ask, 'How do I know? Life is wildly unpredictable and so it would be unwise to make any plans.' All of these are things I've certainly thought at times too – particularly with young children running around, who tend to pick up a multitude of bugs over winter no matter what precautions are taken.

What we fail to see with an approach like this is that every mountain is climbed through a series of small steps. And so, yes, if you left your 90-day goal until the last week, then I could understand why you'd feel a little stretched for time and be left believing it's impossible. If, however, day one of 90 started today with something small, you could well be on track for hitting a big milestone in 89 days' time – even in the uncertainty and even with a hundred other things to do. Our tendency to put off tasks like this goes back to what I said at the start of this section regarding our default mode being reactionary. It takes far more discipline to do the non-urgent but important things today when you have countless other demands seemingly screaming at you.

That's where the belief part of expectation can be really helpful to harness. This is partly found in something called intrinsic motivation.

Intrinsic motivation

When we are extrinsically motivated, we're driven to perform because we want the reward we'll get when we succeed or we want to avoid the punishment we'll get if we don't. Intrinsic motivation, however, is rooted in us achieving purely because we either enjoy the activity we're participating in, or at the very least, are willing to learn lessons through our participation in it. Essentially, the reward is in the activity itself as opposed to what we hope to get while participating in it.

We cannot always be intrinsically motivated. There will always be some tasks which we simply have no desire to participate in whatsoever, and yet participate in them we must. But this doesn't have to be the view we always take when it comes to how we engage in what we do.

The reason I link belief with intrinsic motivation is because there's something about each that leaves room for wonder, hope and curiosity. 'If I do X, I wonder what might happen,' for example, as opposed to

'I have to do X because if I don't, I'll be reprimanded.' This isn't about making ourselves believe that we really love something which we, in fact, cannot stand. Rather, it's allowing ourselves enough time to really reflect on the goal at hand – whether it's one we've been given or one we've set for ourselves. And then it's to ask ourselves whether there's anything about it we could enjoy or learn from as we walk towards achieving it. In a sense, it's about taking ownership of the goal as opposed to giving up before we've even begun.

So, back to the goals I shared at the beginning of this chapter. Why did I struggle with the idea of following through on my revision plan and yet, despite not especially enjoying exercise and very much liking my sleep, I was almost excited by my 6.00 am wake-ups to exercise before my wedding and my late nights on my laptop in the early days of my business? Having now been a teacher myself, I have come to realise the importance of ownership. At 15 years old, I already knew which subjects I liked and disliked. I also, either consciously or sub-consciously, zoned out somewhat when it came to doing work I didn't enjoy. Something we've been talking through with my son, who just started school, is the notion that 'practice makes progress' as opposed to 'practice makes perfect'. He loves maths, and he loves getting the answers right, which he often does, as he's good at it. However, we've had to actively affirm his efforts even when he doesn't get the answers right, as well as encouraging him to expand his areas of effort beyond only what he likes to do. Otherwise, his commitment to or effort in things for which he won't necessarily be rewarded may wane. This sort of approach to interests for ourselves can also be hugely helpful.

The Pomodoro method

Most of us will have the sort of working lives where at least a bit of extrinsic motivation is required: those times where we just need to 'suck it up' and get on with the task at hand. For those moments, I thoroughly recommend the Pomodoro method.

In the late 1980s, Francesco Cirrilo decided he needed a way to become less overwhelmed in the face of his looming university studies. Essentially a form of time blocking, the idea is to work in 25-minute chunks and then take a five-minute break; and to continue this cycle for as long as you need to. It's been proven to benefit countless people in focusing on their tasks and can be especially helpful for those who are neurodivergent and live with ADHD or autism, for example. The tendencies these minds can have towards hyperfocus or even time blindness can be heavily supported by using the Pomodoro method.

So, when intrinsic motivation isn't possible and you have a goal you need to meet regardless, try on the Pomodoro method for size. There are a number of online timers you can use for this method, but honestly, any timer works. The word 'pomodoro' is Italian for tomato and the reason this famous technique got its name is because when first using it, Cirrilo would use a tomato-shaped timer to time his 25-minute study blocks. Use whatever you have!

Faith focus: 'Whatever you do, whether in work or deed…'

Sometimes in the car with my children, we'll listen to kids' worship music together. One of the songs which seems to be repeated a lot has lyrics which recite over and over again, 'Whatever you do, whether in work or deed, do it all for the name of the Lord Jesus.' These lyrics are inspired by Colossians 3:23–24: 'Whatever you do, work at it with all your heart, as working for the Lord, not for human masters, since you know that you will receive an inheritance from the Lord as a reward. It is the Lord Christ you are serving.' Explaining to a four-year-old what these words mean was surprisingly tricky, but I gave it my best shot, saying that even if people aren't quick to give us feedback and praise, the most important reason we're working so hard or putting maximum effort into what we do is because God sees it.

This brought me back once again to my days as a teacher and to the importance of intrinsic motivation. As Christians, we have a greater driver than anyone else to work with a clear vision, even if the work in question isn't something we're completely relishing and thriving in. There were certain terms during my years as a teacher where I had a line manager who perhaps didn't quite get me or who rubbed me up the wrong way with disparaging comments about some of the students I worked with. There were days I truly didn't want to go to work. The silver lining here, however, is that I was able to remind myself of this verse and of the fact that I wasn't doing this work for a boss or for any external reward (don't get me wrong, that would have been nice). The truth is, I felt called to that work at that time. And with a bit of prayer, I was not only able to recentre my focus, but also to remind myself of some of the aspects of the work I was thankful for.

What I did next is one of the most important aspects when it comes to goals, and it is part of the reason I coined it 'expectation' within the TIME framework. A goal like 'Support X with their GCSE English, getting them to complete a mock paper' doesn't sound especially exciting. However, reframing and rephrasing this goal as an affirmation, and indeed an expectation, was a complete game-changer for me. Being able to declare 'I am called to support X in taking a small step towards their future academic success' allowed me to, one, recognise the importance of the work I was doing and, two, reframe something seemingly small into, quite rightly, something of significance.

> I believe that declaring our expectations protects us from pessimism.

Whether these declarations are rooted in the truth of what you're doing or grounded in scripture which speaks to the truth of what you're doing being important to the Lord, they truly will help you. For example, 'Both my public and behind-the-scenes work and effort is seen and rewarded by the Lord' (taken from our Colossians passage).

Proverbs 16:3 states: 'Commit to the Lord whatever you do, and he will establish your plans.' What's especially interesting about this word 'commit' is the fact it's taken from the Hebrew root word *gâlal*, which means 'to roll'. Viewing it in this way makes the verse come to life in pictorial form. Imagine the hard stuff you're holding pertaining to your work, your goals and your expectations, and then imagine bundling it all up (I'm visualising a hay bale here!) and rolling it over to God to take care of. This verse doesn't take away the responsibility we have to do the work. However, there's something about it which removes the pressure of holding tightly to the outcome, because once we've rolled it over to the Lord, he will do what he wants to do. This sentiment of God establishing the plans we set for ourselves is echoed in Proverbs 16:9, but again we do well to notice the part which is recognised as our responsibility – in this case to prayerfully plan the goals, which start as the cry of our hearts. The beauty of both these passages is the fact that we don't need to hold too tightly to the outcome, because it is God who will establish the path we need to take as we trust and lean into his divine leading.

Continuing this whistle-stop tour of Proverbs, we arrive at 19:21: 'Many are the plans in a person's heart, but it is the Lord's purpose that prevails.' When it comes to goals and expectations, I truly value this verse, as it serves as a reminder that we can't really go wrong as believers here. Yes, we can dream, we can plan and we can prayerfully look to the future. It's important to note that there's nothing wrong with that. However, the really good news is that what God wills and wants for us will be what eventually prevails. Don't let the uncertainty of your vision and your hopes put you off from taking action. He has gone before you.

Food for thought

1   Do you typically have a plan of action when it comes to meeting your goals, or do you tend to set a goal and then struggle to take steps towards it? Reading this chapter, are you any more clear on why this might be?

2   Do you find you are more typically extrinsically or intrinsically motivated? How has this helped or hindered the relationship you have with your goals thus far in your personal and professional life?

3   Could you try reframing some of your goals into declarations of expectation? How does doing this change your perspective and outlook on the work you're doing?

6

Wellbeing and gratitude (T)

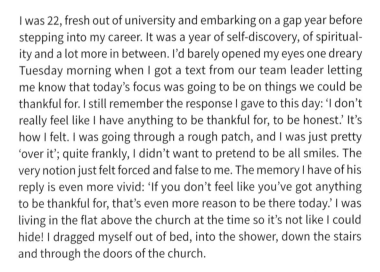

I was 22, fresh out of university and embarking on a gap year before stepping into my career. It was a year of self-discovery, of spirituality and a lot more in between. I'd barely opened my eyes one dreary Tuesday morning when I got a text from our team leader letting me know that today's focus was going to be on things we could be thankful for. I still remember the response I gave to this day: 'I don't really feel like I have anything to be thankful for, to be honest.' It's how I felt. I was going through a rough patch, and I was just pretty 'over it'; quite frankly, I didn't want to pretend to be all smiles. The very notion just felt forced and false to me. The memory I have of his reply is even more vivid: 'If you don't feel like you've got anything to be thankful for, that's even more reason to be there today.' I was living in the flat above the church at the time so it's not like I could hide! I dragged myself out of bed, into the shower, down the stairs and through the doors of the church.

What followed was an exercise in prayer where we laid a grain of rice on the floor one after another in a line, each grain representing something we were thankful for. The aim was for this line of rice to be as long as possible. Trust me, I was eye-rolling pretty hard at the concept, as I'm sure you are right now. My attitude had certainly not caught up with my actions at this point. What transpired, though, was an opportunity to truly reflect, to allow myself to be dug out of the trench I happened to find myself in and remind myself that, yes, even amid the relative sadness I was feeling at that time, there were still things to be thankful for. What transpired was a pretty long rice line and a lot more that I was grateful for than I had first thought.

As cliché as 'an attitude of gratitude' might sound, without one, stinking thinking and negativity creep in, rear their ugly heads and steer us completely off course and straight into pity parties where we get to fan the flames of our frustration.

I was grateful for the opportunity to lift my head above the parapet that day and, to my surprise, find peace and perseverance shifting the pity and pain which had been residing just a few hours prior. Gratitude was a gift to me then, and it's one which keeps on giving.

Digging deeper

The personal development world is keen to tell us about the benefits of positivity. Even dipping your toe in that way of thinking makes you aware that there's no getting away from the notion that 'an attitude of gratitude' is one of the key ingredients when it comes to succeeding in life and work. Having worked as a coach for years, often acquiring information and insight from thought leaders who wouldn't necessarily profess to be Christians, but would certainly bang the gratitude drum, I found myself nodding in agreement to a lot of the ideas they presented.

This can often be where a lot of Christians disengage, suggesting that this way of thinking comes across as 'wishy washy' or even New Age. While there are certainly some real issues to unpack with 'toxic positivity', which we're about to dive into, we can't get away from the fact that gratitude is important to God. This is worth remembering for two reasons. First, because as Christians we can sometimes synonymise obedience to God with a lack of joy or thankfulness. Second, because when those who don't know God see Christians living out gratitude, it will hopefully shed some light on the difference knowing God makes to life.

Philippians 4:6 says: 'Do not be anxious about anything, but in every situation, by prayer and petition, with thanksgiving, present your requests to God.' This verse is crucial to our correct understanding of gratitude. The fact that Paul is urging us to not be anxious about anything suggests that those he's talking to are indeed allowing worry to creep in. Why else would he be telling them not to be anxious? The verse goes on to share that in *every* situation, both prayerfully and with *thanksgiving*, we're to give these petitions over to God. I can't be the only one who has sometimes prayed through gritted teeth and an attitude of 'should' as opposed to joy, acknowledging the fact that no matter my circumstances, I can boldly approach the God of the universe for help. This means that while I might not be at all grateful for the circumstances I am experiencing (this isn't about pretending everything's fine), I can be thankful for the fact that the God of the heavens and the earth, the one who flung the stars into space almost as an afterthought (see Genesis 1:16), is with me and for me, no matter what.

Our 'Faith focus' for this chapter will explore the damaging effects of holding an opposing attitude to one of gratitude, taking a look at 2 Timothy 3. We'll also dive a little deeper into something I outlined in the introduction regarding wellbeing as a whole – it's because of our source that we have it, as opposed to our circumstances. Similarly, the Bible instructs us to give thanks not because of our circumstances but because of who God is in the midst of them. We'll explore what that could look like by looking at 1 Thessalonians 5:18, Psalm 107:1 and 2 Timothy 3:1–9.

Why gratitude?

Although we looked at the 'E' (Expectation) from the TIME framework first, 'Thankful' is the first pillar of the framework. Gratitude serves as a perspective checker and a way in which to ground ourselves before we get busy with setting our intentions, mapping out our 'me moments' and declaring our expectations. When it comes to busy lives full of work and a myriad of responsibilities and requests, it can be tempting to dive into what needs to be done without checking our hearts and minds first. When we recall what we're thankful for, we approach the potential drudgery of the day with a renewed sense of perspective and focus. As I shared at the start of this chapter, we won't always *feel* thankful. However, there is always something to be thankful for. Remembering this, even and perhaps especially in our challenging moments, can give us pause for thought and potentially even shift the way we're showing up in the other areas of our lives for the better.

All of this aside, it's important to address the dangers of toxic positivity. 'Just be positive, even when you're going through the worst time of your life' isn't what I'm saying here. This is hugely detrimental to our wellbeing. Similarly, all sorts of conflicting emotions can rise to the surface when we think about the sense of gratitude we hold for things going well in our lives, and yet face the sometimes heartbreaking realities of what's happening both for our loved ones and for those all over the world who are suffering. How can gratitude possibly have a place there?

It can be difficult to maintain a grateful disposition against the backdrop of our varied lives. It begs the question, why is it important? The truth of the matter is that our thoughts are going nowhere. We have a greater propensity to unhappiness than we do to happiness, and so it's not surprising that we can so often lean towards thinking about what we and those around us lack than dwell on what we do have and can be thankful for.

The science of gratitude

On his podcast *Huberman Lab*, American neuroscientist and podcaster Dr Andrew Huberman talks about the importance of forming a gratitude practice. He states that 'Gratitude is a mindset which sets the context of your experience such that you can derive tremendous health benefits.'[5] Many of the gratitude practices he goes on to discuss involve receiving gratitude, as opposed to only giving it, and it is these which have the most long-lasting effects. Of course, waiting around to be thanked isn't exactly the most beneficial use of our time. However, it's scientifically significant that viewing someone receiving gratitude can have almost the same effect.

I must admit that when I heard about this, something I've wondered about myself for years was finally confirmed. Whenever I watch a televised talent show such as *The X Factor* or *Britain's Got Talent*, I often watch with anticipation when the unassuming individual nervously takes the stage. I then almost always find myself covered in goosebumps and welling up when the most remarkable talent comes out of this individual and brings the audience to their feet in rapturous applause. In my study of gratitude, I'm led to believe that my emotion at these scenes is a direct result of my neural circuitry reacting to these people receiving gratitude and appreciation for their talent and hard work. This would certainly be backed up by the science which indicates that when our gratitude practice is rooted in story, it's even more powerful – and everyone knows how well those TV shows tell the backstory of their contestants.

In one of my coaching sessions with a client, she was discussing her working relationship with her team. My client's team were all very different to her in terms of leadership style, and one of her goals as a manager was to be able to effectively support them all, collectively and individually. At one point during our session, she mentioned one team member who always just 'got on with it', but never seemed to ask for feedback and also didn't receive much, as she always had her head down working. There were some awards which came up in her sector and my client nominated this team member, sharing a glowing recommendation as to why they deserved it. Once my client's team member realised she'd received this, she sent a lengthy response of thanks back to my client explaining how much it meant to her to hear those words. On our call, my client gleefully exclaimed, 'The joy is in the giving.' She spoke about the fact that sharing this expression of gratitude and appreciation broke through a type of wall and enabled her to realise how good it felt to celebrate other people's success, recognising they're humans too, no matter how unbothered they appear about feedback or how little they appear to desire it.

As I mentioned, waiting around to receive gratitude is a highly self-indulgent waste of time. However, the good news is that by showing our appreciation of others, we get to play a significant role in seeing how gratitude shapes them. Not only this, though. As Christians, while it might be a stretch to say that God is grateful for us, we can certainly say with confidence that he loves us unconditionally and delights in us. Considering that he does not shift or change depending on mood or emotion, we can be thankful that this love and delight is truly a constant.

Faith focus: When thankfulness doesn't thrive

We don't have to do too much digging, both in faith-based circles and otherwise, to find multiple studies, books and journals centred around the notion of gratitude. The regularity with which we see the reminders of it could leave us with the idea that it's simply something we can pick up and put down based on how we feel and what's going on that day.

There are countless moments in scripture that point to the importance God places on gratitude, with many passages centred around money and giving to the church. For example, 2 Corinthians 9:7 notes that

'God loves a cheerful giver'. Although this passage is certainly about money, it goes without saying that when gratitude is given both to people and to God freely and cheerfully, as opposed to bitterly through gritted teeth, it is received much more warmly.

But what about those instances where, quite frankly, life is awful? Where we're walking through incredibly dark times, uncertain of how we'll ever be able to emerge with utterances of gratitude? Are we truly supposed to give thanks then?

God is not shocked or surprised by our circumstances. This doesn't mean that he condones our mistreatment and suffering. We don't have to look too far into Jesus' life to understand that, fully God and fully man, he empathised with human sorrow (John 11:35; Luke 19:41; Hebrews 5:7–9). But it does mean that the command to give thanks isn't given only for those who have obvious external reason to do so. Psalm 107:1 opens with a call to 'Give thanks to the Lord'. The verse goes on to say: 'For he is good; his love endures forever.' Even when life isn't good, he is. Even when we feel as though we can't go on, by his enduring and loving presence in our lives, we can. The reason gratitude is important to God, and should therefore be important to us as believers, is not because of who we are or what we're going through, but rather because of who he is and what he went through on the cross in order that we might live.

1 Thessalonians 5:18 says: 'Give thanks in all circumstances; for this is God's will for you in Christ Jesus.' Here, we see thanksgiving go beyond a nice idea or something to add into prayer when we feel like it, but rather, God's will for us. God doesn't make mistakes or say things for no good reason, so it's important for us to investigate why it would be his will for us to give thanks.

The verses which precede 1 Thessalonians 5:18 speak of 'rejoicing' and 'praying', which are likely included in 'this is God's will' alongside thankfulness. The Greek word translated as 'rejoice' here is *chairō*, which describes being 'full of cheer' or even 'calmly happy'. Again, in the face of trial, the notion of cheer seems a little peculiar. However, what this points to is how we as believers are to be distinguished. Not by excitement and happiness because things have gone our way, but by a sure and certain steadiness of temperament, even when they haven't. This is not a temperament which suggests that everything is fine when it's not. Rather, it is one which holds wholeheartedly to the understanding that we know who is holding us through it all. This is what I believe is meant by giving thanks being God's will for us. In Christ, gratitude is a disposition which isn't predicated upon a particular destination.

2 Timothy 3:1–9 contains a lot of warnings about the last days. Timothy is given a long list of things to be on the lookout for and interestingly enough, among themes such as abuse and greed, is ingratitude (v. 2). The passage goes on to talk about people who possess these traits as having 'a form of godliness, but denying its power' (v. 5). Again, I believe that these verses point to what is essentially a supernatural ability to be grateful to God purely because of who he is. When we are so hidden in him, our hearts and minds so changed by him, we – like the woman who anointed Jesus' feet with perfume and wiped them with her hair (Matthew 26:6–13) – will have no choice but to humble ourselves before him in thanksgiving.

This isn't always easy, and God knows this. He knows our frame and remembers we are but dust (Psalm 103:14). But when we're faith-filled enough to give him this gratitude in spite of everything else, we can be certain it will not return to us void.

Food for thought

1   If you were honest with yourself, how much time would you say you spend focusing on what you lack or are struggling with, as opposed to what you have and are grateful for? Why is that?

2   What are you taking in from relationships, social media, TV, etc. that is contributing to finding gratitude difficult to cultivate? Are you paying attention to how much you're feeding that? In contrast to this, what or who are you surrounding yourself with that does provoke a sense of gratitude within you?

3   Can you think of a time when you have received real gratitude for something you've done? How does reflecting on this instance cause you to feel? Is this something you could make a habit of by way of contribution to your own gratitude practice?

7

Wellbeing and productivity (I)

Have you ever kicked off your year with a word? If you have, perhaps you'll be familiar with the way it unfolds. You think about the type of theme you want your year to have, and then you pick a word which anchors that theme.

In 2019, my word was 'intentional'.

I also started 2019 about five months pregnant with my first child.

I didn't think that one of these things would be a problem for the other, but I must say my pregnancy and my word for that year quite often butted heads.

If I'd been thinking about intention in the way I've taught it for years, and the way it's now integrated with the Time & Pace® framework, there wouldn't have been an issue. But as I'm sure you know all too well, we can quite often be slower to heed our own advice than we are to give it.

You see, long before I even taught it, I often thought that intentionality should be pointed in the direction of what your heart and mind is suggesting first. Now of course, with this train of thought, many of us could say that our hearts and minds are leading us to our streaming service of choice, a bowl of popcorn and our pyjamas. As nice as that sounds, it's not quite what I mean.

If you are indeed someone who daily feels the pull to a box set and PJs, I want to ask you: when was the last time you felt excited by your 'normal' day to day? The last time you woke up feeling invigorated or, at the very least, enthused about what you had laid in front of you to do?

I ask because, if truth be told, we're created to work. Now, your work may well look different to mine. Your work might be a 9–5, night shifts, running a business, home educating your children, working in an office, running around after your pre-schoolers all day, volunteering and charity work, or anything else in between. Whatever work looks like for you, I'm sure that:

1 You can remember a time you were last energised and excited about doing it, whether that's today or ten years ago.
2 You'd like to feel like that more often.

I was a teacher for seven years, and although I had occasional days of excitement throughout my career, after the first couple of years I couldn't get enough 'rest' – even after a six-week summer holiday, even after being super-organised and knowing exactly what I should be doing that day/week, and even after a promotion and more responsibility being offered to me.

You see, as intentional as I decided to be about my day to day, I'd find that, eventually, none of it would be as fulfilling as I'd hoped, because it simply wasn't me any longer. The irritability I noticed at not being able to feel accomplished in my role was because I thought that I should feel better than I was when doing the work I'd been given to do. In a moment, I'll be talking about the well-known parable of the talents. For those familiar with the story, remember the third servant's response to being entrusted with a part of his master's life savings? He buried what was given to him because of fear. For so long, I buried the thought that I could move on and carve out a different career for myself as I held on tightly to fear and the fact that teaching had been all I'd really known.

It's time to shed the 'should'.

'Should' forces you into boxes you weren't built for.

'Should' causes you to second-guess your heart's desires.

'Should' makes you question and compare way more than is necessary.

If, during my late pregnancy and early motherhood, I'd recognised that where I needed to be intentional was with my son and with myself – healing and getting to know who I now was – then any other work I did would have been a great bonus. Instead, despite being on a form of maternity leave, my lack of social media posts, programme launches and online presence nudged at me accusingly at the end of every day, trying to tell me where I hadn't met the mark somehow.

If I'd realised, or in this case, stopped ignoring, the fact that teaching was no longer the career for me, I'd have chosen to start looking elsewhere for work and would have remained in gratitude for my present, trusting that it would serve a purpose for my future. I'd have recognised that the feelings of flatness week after week, despite my best efforts, were a nudge to move on to pastures new and to be intentional there as opposed to a suggestion that I should force myself that little bit more, as though that would change anything.

What if our intentions began with our intuition?

What if those nudges from the Holy Spirit as we do and as we dream are something to take hold of and run with?

Digging deeper

Many of us will be familiar with the parable of the talents which Jesus told in Matthew 25:14–30. I've always found this story fascinating, and it speaks to the area of productivity quite clearly.

Here is a master, leaving town on a very long journey. He entrusts his life savings and then some (a talent was worth what a day labourer would earn across 20 years) to three of his servants. The first thing which always strikes me about this parable is that each was given talents in accordance with their ability. Although the common phrase 'God will never give you more than you can handle' isn't actually in the Bible, the notion that we're equal in worth and yet different in our abilities is a fact. One servant gets five talents, another two and the last, one.

The servants all do different things with their talents, which we'll address in a moment. When the master returns, the first two have essentially doubled their money, while the last one hasn't seen any growth at all. In fact, he buried what was given out of fear.

How often do we bury what God's given to us, either physically or spiritually, because of fear? How often do we get anxious about whether or not it was actually God who said X or called us to Y, and in our hesitation and doubt, find ourselves shrinking back? I know I certainly relate to that third servant at times.

Back to the first and second servants, though. The master's pleasure in their activity was exactly the same. This is further evidence that 'doing the most' isn't what's rewarded, but rather, productively stewarding whatever it is that's been given. Note, though, that productive stewardship doesn't automatically mean overexerting yourself to the point of burnout. The admonition that the master gives the third servant (see v. 27) is that even investing the talent so that it would have at least made some interest would have been better than simply burying it and leaving it to do nothing. If the man had done this, it wouldn't have taken much physical exertion from him but still would have produced fruitful results.

How, then, do we diligently and productively steward what God has entrusted us with, without it meaning burnout and a lack of boundaries? Our 'Faith focus' for this chapter will explore John 15, which has a lot to say about just that.

To do, or not to do?

For longer than I'd like to admit, I was someone with what you'd call an 'all or nothing' mentality. Beyond simply taking pride in my work, there was also an aspect of getting something done well, meaning that you were inevitably going to sacrifice other aspects of life in order to do so. Contrary to some of the self-care and wellbeing gurus we come across, I'm not here to state that you never have to work a day in your life in order to achieve the success you seek. However, I will categorically say that organising your priorities must absolutely come before organising your productivity. To unpack this idea a little more, I'll take you back to when I was just starting out with my coaching business.

I'd started an online community for faith-first female entrepreneurs, where I'd show up and share thoughts, journal prompts and training. I'd also share ways in which they could work with me in this community. Much to my delight, things started taking off quickly, which essentially left me biting off more than I could chew. In theory, I could physically take on all that was being thrown at me. If I looked at the hours available, I could 'technically' coach several clients a day, several days a week. And so I did. But what I hadn't factored in to my not-so-careful carving out within my calendar was margin time. Margin time for rest and reflection, sure, but also margin time for planning, preparation and regular vision-casting and vision check-ins. If you're constantly on the go, these things don't happen. From the outside looking in, though, it looks like you've never been more productive.

At what cost?

For me, it's only been recently that I've realised how significant the cost was. Some things were more easily recognisable at the time – basic self-care coming last, for example, as well as a lack of boundaries in place, all in the name of a job well done, which quite frankly looked a lot like people-pleasing over an actual good job. Something deeper, however, was my attitude towards the work itself. As someone who had spent years volunteering at and leading youth groups and women's ministries, I'd always enjoyed mentoring people. When I realised that coaching was a viable profession, I leapt at the opportunity. What this boundary-free season had done for that zeal, though, was somehow to quench it. You see, a lack of margin and an absence of boundaries will have you believing that something meant for you is actually anything but.

When I began my executive coaching and mentoring qualification a few months after my daughter was born, I was absolutely astounded at how much I enjoyed coaching the clients I had to practise with in order to get enough evidenced hours of coaching. It was like I fell in love with the work all over again. What was very different this time, however, was the two young children I now had and the fact that I could no longer afford to burn the candle at both ends, nor did I want to. In all honesty, I couldn't afford to do this the first time either. But putting up a boundary when you don't technically have to takes a lot more strength than adhering to the ones which are put up for you because of circumstances, doesn't it?

Parkinson's Law

In fact, it's often not completely our fault when we find ourselves filling all the time we have with tasks and to-do lists. Parkinson's Law would argue that we're wired this way. In an essay for *The Economist* in 1955, historian and author Cyril Northcote Parkinson wrote: 'It is a commonplace observation that work expands so as to fill the time available for its completion.'[6]

When he wrote that essay's opening line, he probably didn't realise that it would take on a life of its own and become something people hold fast to today. Because we do, don't we? It's why so many people burn the midnight oil the night before their dissertation or something similar is due, despite knowing that this deadline would come for months prior. Whether we're given a deadline or create one ourselves, even the most organised among us might struggle not to fill all the time given as opposed to giving the task as long as it takes.

Does this mean that giving ourselves shorter timelines in order to get work done would improve our productivity? Not necessarily.

Take this book and what I shared in the introduction. I started writing it much later than the day I signed the contract. I ummed and ahhed about my ability to write a book on such a topic. I prayed, I questioned myself, I even questioned God. However, eventually, I got to work and completed the manuscript. The evidence is what you're holding now. I can't say that I knew I'd have the sort of feelings I had when I first began to write (and I'm very glad I had them, as they uncovered such truth). But I do know a little about the way I work and the way people work in general. So, when I was asked when I'd be able to submit this work, I gave myself a little more time than I perhaps needed. I gave myself a margin. A margin for children's sick days and a baby at home with me. A margin for unexpected meetings and urgent emails. I gave myself a margin for prayerful preparation. This was not work I wanted to rush, nor panic about. To write a book about work–life wellbeing in that state would be fairly hypocritical.

So, *could* we collectively get our work completed faster? Could we become even more efficient and, dare I say, robot-like, so that more could get done in less time? Probably. With the rise of artificial intelligence (AI), we're already being given the tools for this to happen. That's not all bad, of course. AI can offer some the ability to work smarter as opposed to harder. However, when it comes to work which requires our own manual efforts, squeezing more out of our already stretched selves is not the answer. Despite what we've been led to think about it, productivity isn't the same as panic, push and pressure, and yet, when we're having a busy day, we might name each of those emotional states and call the day a productive one. What could it take to rethink and redo this way of walking through the world?

A question to consider when you're next asked how quickly you'll be able to get something done:

 Do I want this to be rushed or do I want this to be right?

As important as our work is, as I've outlined here, our approach to how we get it done could be challenged in order to allow for us to think about the bigger picture – to think about our whole lives (with our work as a big part of that), as opposed to the rest of our lives being given whatever's left once the work is done. So with that, let's talk about intangible goals. These are goals that are dependent on factors over which you have no control, such as other people, biology or even the weather. Don't ignore or squash down those desires in the name of productivity, as though having them is a distraction. Don't neglect to write down those things too as you're mapping out your next week, month, quarter or year. Those goals are just as important as the ones you're paid to reach, even if society, peer pressure or an angry manager tells you otherwise.

We hear so much about SMART goals that it causes us to think that if goal-setting doesn't look like this, we're just shooting arrows into the wind and hoping for the best. I would like to think otherwise. Of course, when a goal has a deadline, there is the time-bound element to it, which means that we need to prioritise what steps we'll take to get there and when we'll take them. I've spoken a little bit about how I believe those steps can be taken in a way which doesn't promote unnecessary pressure. However, not every goal is time-bound (I'm thinking about those intangibles we can't control), and it's with that in mind that I like to round up our thoughts about goals more from the perspective of 'BHAGs'. Originally coined by Jim Collins, BHAGs represent 'big hairy audacious goals'.[7]

As I've taken a chapter of this book to explain, I believe that mindset is fundamentally the key to so much of our success. BHAGs cause us to stretch our thinking and believe beyond what is possible and tangible only in the here and now. This is important because, as the famous quote goes, 'Shoot for the moon and if you miss, at least you'll land among the stars.' As glib as this might sound, there's some truth to it. If we only ever think about goals in ways that are specific and measurable, then we'll rarely, if ever, give ourselves the opportunity to dream big, because we'll tell ourselves what's not possible and will therefore potentially limit ourselves in the process.

My goal with Time & Pace® is for you to keep going and to keep growing in a way which makes sense for *you* and your *whole* life. So with that, ahead of our 'Faith focus', here are some questions for you to consider:

- Do any of the goals you have for the next 90 days have nothing to do with work?
- Where are you allowing those goals (if you have them) to fall in your list of priorities?
- What boundaries can you put in place to protect those goals?
- How will making time for those goals help you to show up differently (and more powerfully) in areas of your life going forwards?

Faith focus: abiding – where true productivity begins

In her book *The Best Yes*, Lysa TerKeurst says: 'A woman who lives with the stress of an overwhelmed schedule will often ache with the sadness of an underwhelmed soul.'[8] I wonder if you relate to these words in the same way as I have in seasons past? I wonder if the stress of your schedule can sometimes feel overwhelming, and yet you maintain the pressure to keep it that way, all in the name of productivity or performance-based metrics?

What are you doing to and for your soul in those moments? How can we change this in a society which continually asks for more from us?

We read that as Christians, we'll be known by our fruit (see Matthew 7:15–20). So, some might argue, it makes sense, is biblical even, to do the most in order to be seen the most. However, in John 15, Jesus describes himself as 'the true vine' and his Father as the gardener, or vine dresser. In verses 1–8, he reiterates the fact that without him, our efforts are futile. For example, verse 4: 'Remain in me, as I also remain in you. No branch can bear fruit by itself; it must remain in the vine. Neither can you bear fruit unless you remain in me.'

This word 'remain', or 'abide' as other translations render it, is taken from the Greek root word *menō*. Meaning to stay, stand or dwell, it's about the disposition of our soul. We remain in Christ through the reading of his word, through prayer and through worship. Have we ever properly considered, though, that without these things, we're clutching at straws?

The premise of this book is that wellbeing has much more to do with our source than our circumstances, and this passage really drives that point home from the perspective of productivity. With Jesus at the helm of our plans and our goals, we're reminded that we're not only a body, but rather a whole being. Here we're reminded that we're also a soul and a spirit and that those parts of us matter just as much as, if not more than, our physical nature.

Rather than trying to do everything in our own strength and then go to God for his sign-off blessing, this portion of scripture is a reminder to go to him first, to dwell there, to seek his guidance and wisdom before deciding that we know best. Verses 7–8 reassure us of this: 'If you remain in me and my words remain in you, ask whatever you wish, and it will be done for you. This is to my Father's glory, that you bear much fruit, showing yourselves to be my disciples.'

The work itself isn't where we're going wrong; it's where we're working from which sometimes misses the mark and causes us to bite off more than we can chew – perhaps because we're trying to dine at tables that are not ours to sit at.

Food for thought

1 What boundaries have you recently put up around your time, talents and treasure, which you've done because you've wanted to as opposed to having to? If this isn't something you're familiar with, consider where you'd like to do this.

2 What's one BHAG you'd like to focus on for the next 90 days?

3 Where have you been working from your own strength in the name of productivity? What might it look like to abide instead, and be shown what to pick up and what to put down? How can you make provision for that?

8

Wellbeing and real self-care (M)

It was a summer afternoon in July and I'd finally carved out the time to sit with the expectations page of my Time Journal® to map out my goals for the next 90 days. It was only when I got to the end of the list of ten goals that I realised not one of them was related to work. Had this been me a few years back, almost every goal would be related to my business, no matter how the rest of my life looked at the time or what I wanted outside of work. Back then, those things would have been at the bottom of the list, if indeed they'd made the list at all.

On that July afternoon, I knew that I needed time and space over the next 90 days to heal, to rest, to recharge and to be creative in private as opposed to public – to regroup and to be restored. Your first thought when you hear a notion like this might be to roll your eyes, gesturing towards the fact that you don't have time to think about necessities like these in the midst of such a busy schedule. Of course, the truth of the matter is that barely anyone does. 'Spare' time doesn't tend to be the norm, does it? But things that are as important as healing and health – mentally, physically, spiritually and emotionally – have to have time *carved out* for them. It's not going to suddenly appear or be 'fitted in' unless they are made a priority.

So I must admit, I was quite emotional when I realised that, without thinking about it, I'd mapped myself out ten goals which didn't look like work or business for a change. Did setting these ten goals, which looked so different to goals that I've set previously, mean that I did no work at all? Of course not. I, like so many others, not only need to work but also *want* to. Work is something we're wired for – whatever work looks like for you. But the fact that my focus wasn't fixated solely on my output was something to celebrate that day.

The Oxford English Dictionary defines goal as 'the object of a person's ambition or effort; an aim or desired outcome'. Having desires and dreams which fall outside of our productivity and effort doesn't mean that we won't work and that we'll become so out of touch with reality that we forget what it's like to actually put effort in in order to obtain results. As I've said, that's not how we're wired. So we don't need to worry that everything we've subconsciously learned will disappear overnight. However, bringing your intentions around personal wellness and self-care to the fore will mean you might just pay attention to these in the midst of your busy days, weeks and months. Thinking in this way, though, is a muscle which will need training, just as you trained your brain in other ways during years of compulsory education and beyond.

I knew what I wanted to achieve during the months of July, August and September – and to be honest with you, 'achievement' might be the wrong word here – but these expectations didn't mean that work stopped in its tracks. In fact, sometimes work and the creative process of my writing and journalling was part of what enabled me to think through some of the aims and objectives that I had for the future. That said, recognising and remembering those aims that I'd written down on 1 July meant that when I found myself steering off course and heading down a rabbit hole of 'success' meaning doing more, I had something to anchor myself back to. I had reminders of my desires, which caused me to think and do differently.

Digging deeper

It might seem strange to start a chapter supposedly focused on 'real self-care' by talking more about goals and expectations, albeit through a different lens. However, things won't change until we do. Until we can get to the root of the fact that the entirety of our lives doesn't need to revolve around producing more, lasting change will be challenging.

In fact, real self-care begins with your mind and emotions. There's no point in having a monthly massage if, throughout it, you're plagued with worry and guilt over what you *could* be doing instead of lying there. While the self-care industry of mani-pedis, massages and mojitos is all well and good, if we don't address why we can't enjoy these things in the first place, we'll stay stuck.

In 1 Peter 3, Peter addresses wives specifically and talks about where the source of their beauty should come from. It's not the hair, make-up and outfits which so many of us today place such emphasis on (not that wanting to look good is a sin, by the way – we've heard far too much of that from the church over the years). What Peter describes as essentially the source of beauty is in verse 4: 'Rather, it should be that of your inner self, the unfading beauty of a gentle and quiet spirit, which is of great worth in God's sight.' When I first looked at this and acknowledged the fact that I'm not the quietest of humans, I must say it irked me somewhat. However, digging a little deeper into the text, I was interested to find that this notion of a quiet spirit comes from the Greek root word *hēsuchios*, which can be derived as being undisturbed and peaceable. This word is only used one other time in the Bible, in 1 Timothy 2:2, when Paul is urging prayer so that the church 'may live peaceful and quiet lives in all godliness and holiness'. This quiet and peaceable disposition isn't about sitting pretty and speaking only when spoken to, but rather, it's about our inner lives and what that comes to be outwardly. Knowing who and whose we are changes everything, including the way in which we take care of ourselves spiritually, physically, mentally and emotionally, and also in how we choose to present ourselves to the outside world as a result.

What if real self-care was all about the inner game before anything external was explored? Our 'Faith focus' for this chapter will look at Matthew 6:25–34 as we explore worry and what it's actually doing to either help or hinder our day-to-day lives.

The basics of the brain

In his book *Change Your Brain, Change Your Life*, Daniel Amen says:

> Your brain is involved in everything you do and everything you are, including how you think, how you feel, how you act, and how well you get along with other people. Your brain is the organ behind your intelligence, character and every single decision you make.[9]

Hippocrates put it like this: 'I am of the opinion that the brain exercises the greatest power in the man.'[10]

The part of the brain that most effectively helps us to form habits is called the 'basal ganglia'. The basal ganglia is also a contributing factor to setting our anxiety levels. Amen and his team have scanned over 250,000 brains and have found that people who have anxious tendencies or disorders tend to have an overactive basal ganglia, meaning that they are more likely to be overwhelmed by stressful situations and have a tendency to freeze in thought or action when these scenarios arise.

If this part of the brain is also where we're forming habit loops, I wonder if those of us with an overactive basal ganglia might also be prone to forming habits which further stoke our naturally anxious tendencies? This isn't always something we can stop simply because we want to, of course. There can be times where we experience such crippling anxiety that it's hard for us to think about anything else. However, real self-care, I believe, is about acknowledging the critical importance of paying attention to our thoughts and feelings when we do feel able to. In fact, in 2 Corinthians 10:5, the Bible describes this as taking your thoughts captive. As we've read regarding neuroplasticity, the brain can change shape through the pathways and connections it forms, and so allowing ourselves to believe that we're stuck in any given state isn't strictly true.

It took me a perhaps too hasty sprint out of the starting blocks into the world of work, a diagnosis of depression and anxiety, and a new school later, before I recognised my need to create a little more margin for my mental health and time for anything outside of work. I'd been offered the position of leading our school's equivalent of an alternative education unit, working with a group of students who were removed from the main school for reasons varying from attendance to behaviour. Although this role offered me some of the most rewarding experiences of my career to date, it also gave me some of the most challenging. I remember one day in particular when I stood at the top of the steep staircase leading out of the tiny north London flat my husband and I lived in at the time with tears in my eyes. The day before had been an especially bad day at the school where I was teaching at the time. 'I can't do it,' I murmured to my husband, trying my best (and failing) not to cry.

To be frank, had the school introduced a 'Wellbeing Wednesday', where I got to leave 30 minutes early or something, the chances are it wouldn't have changed much. I'd probably have just ended up taking even more work home and then feeling resentful about it. I'd realised a short time before (in truth, I think I'd known deep down for a while) that teaching was no longer for me. Not because of any one thing in particular. I loved my students and a number of my colleagues, I'd learned a lot and there were times I thoroughly enjoyed it. But for many more reasons than need to be explained here, the career itself was no longer for me.

Have you ever experienced a shift like this – a certainty that you're no longer doing what you're meant to be, and yet you have no clear 'escape route' in sight? Have you ever despondently decided that dissatisfaction is your 'cross to bear', and resigned yourself to the situation you're in?

I wanted to trust God and be obedient. I didn't want to rock the boat. I also wanted to be the best I could be, where I thought I was supposed to be. So, I started looking into doing a Masters and PhD. I bought some books. 'If I've got to be here,' I reasoned, 'I'll be the best and most qualified I can be while I'm doing it.' I wonder if you can relate to that.

Before I share a little about how I eventually left teaching, I want to share what a changed and resolved mind did for my outlook and attitude when it came to the job I still had.

The room I taught in had no windows (no, I'm not sure why either), and my lunch break was usually non-existent because I was still in the building grabbing a sandwich on the job, which may sound familiar to you.

However, I was determined to take some time for me. When I removed the martyr mentality and decided to take ownership of what I *could* change (and believe me, there was a lot I couldn't), I was able to feel more peace and less frustration with my current circumstances, which was transformative for me.

The building above where I taught happened to be a church, and so one day I popped in, explained who I was and the job I had, and asked if I could sit in one of the rooms of the church during my lunch break once or twice a week if I just needed a moment to catch my breath.

They not only said yes, they also gave me a key. What followed was the opportunity for regular 'me moments', however little time I had during a busy work week.

Within the TIME framework, the 'M' stands for 'Me' and encourages you to take a 'me moment' every day, whether that's five minutes or 55 minutes. The Time Journal® explores a little more about what this might look like. To be clear, though, layering a 'me moment' on top of something which is no longer for you is not serving anyone, least of all you. And this is why I say that self-care starts as an inside job. Until you can truly examine your heart and mind regarding where you're at, and if it's somewhere you still want to be or something you still want to be doing, then no holiday, massage or Pilates class will be long enough. Trust me.

It's important to note here that having the option even to think about leaving an environment which is no longer serving you is a luxury that not everyone can entertain. I worked with a client who wanted to leave her job but couldn't for some time for a number of reasons. However, her demeanour and disposition when she realised that's what she wanted meant that she was able to enforce some basic boundaries she hadn't previously, enabling her to take better care of herself while still in a less-than-ideal situation, as opposed to being blown about by every request and requirement she used to rush to meet at the expense of herself.

Another angle to this, of course, might be that you love your job, and leaving it would be the last thing on your mind. It's just that, recently, there have been some less-than-ideal scenarios, which have left you with cause for concern. It's great to be exploring that and considering how and where things might have shifted, so that you can do what's needed in order to get things back on track. Often, it's the slow drift into dissatisfaction which leaves you with a bitter taste in your mouth weeks, months or years down the line, wondering how you got there.

So back to my job as a teacher and how it ended. I never got those extra qualifications and it's a good job too, because a few short (well, agonisingly long) months later, I was made redundant. God clearly had bigger plans for me than I had for myself. I don't *think* he was especially impressed with the elaborate display of martyrdom I'd been showing – it wasn't one he'd asked for! I had just assumed that the rest of my days would be spent living for the weekend and that that was what God had wanted.

I'm not saying that we're not sometimes called to hard things. That's absolutely false, and anyone who tells you we're created purely to thrive without any experience of difficulty or dissatisfaction is lying. John 16:33 tells us in no uncertain terms that we *will* have trouble in this life. This isn't a possibility; it's a promise. So how do we walk between the waiting and the 'what's next', and how does this impact us mentally and emotionally?

Faith focus: look at the birds

It seems fitting that the final chapter before concluding this book takes us back to where we started: in my children's pitch-black bedroom, trying desperately to get one child to sleep while simultaneously doing everything in my power not to wake the other.

When I told God then that I wasn't sure how I was meant to write the very book you're holding, he reminded me that this wasn't about me, but about him. It always has been and always will be.

The self-help and personal development world will continually explain that if we follow X formula, we'll be less stressed, more productive and easier to get along with. While so much of what that world teaches us *is* helpful, the notion that life and the way in which we live it is 'one size fits all' isn't.

I remember first reading Matthew 6:25–34 when I'd returned from university and a life which didn't especially honour God. He found me as a pretty confused 21-year-old, uncertain about what I was going to do with my life next in terms of work, relationships, and even where in the country I'd live. A few weeks later, I had signed up to a gap year with my church, where I'd be living in a flat above the church on only a weekly 'allowance' for food. Outside looking in, it didn't make the most sense for a university graduate with a decent degree to be in this position, but I knew without a shadow of a doubt that it's where God wanted me. One evening service, I'd walked downstairs and into the church building, sat on the carpeted floor as normal and then heard these words spoken as someone approached the microphone with a Bible in hand.

> Therefore I tell you, do not worry about your life, what you will eat or drink; or about your body, what you will wear. Is not life more than food, and the body more than clothes? Look at the birds of the air; they do not sow or reap or store away in barns, and yet your heavenly Father feeds them. Are you not much more valuable than they? Can any one of you by worrying add a single hour to your life?
> MATTHEW 6:25–27

So much of this passage hit home for this recently recommitted Christian; that question in verse 27 in particular. What is to be gained by worrying? How do we benefit? What does it enable, which not taking on that disposition does not? In truth, I couldn't think of much of an answer. Worrying is our brain's natural response to situations we don't like, of course. But to have a question posed regarding who or what it's actually helping certainly gave me pause. It still does.

And so instead of worrying, what *do* we do?

Well, we *know* the basics, don't we? We've read enough Instagram quotes which talk about setting boundaries, getting fresh air, exercising and staying hydrated to know some of the smaller steps we can take in order to look after ourselves. With almost six million people being members of the National Trust, and 11 million being members of a gym, it seems as though quite a few of us at least are outside and exercising more than ever. But the statistics don't lie. In this post-pandemic world, we are a people who are also more anxious than ever. The disconnect is stark.

Jesus' suggestion in Matthew 6 is clear: change our focus. He talks about both the birds and the flowers and calls us to observe how they go about their day-to-day life. In verse 30, he gives us some food for thought regarding where our faith is at:

> If that is how God clothes the grass of the field, which is here today and tomorrow is thrown into the fire, will he not much more clothe you – you of little faith?
> MATTHEW 6:30

If we were, again, to make this less rhetorical and turn this question in on ourselves, how would we honestly answer that question – 'Will he not much more clothe you?'

Well? Will he? Do you believe that?

When does our good work – our worship before God using the gifts he's given us – become an extension of our worry? When do we indeed 'labour or spin' (v. 28), as opposed to leaning on him?

The passage goes on, reassuringly, to state that God knows what we need. Sometimes I think that's the part we find the hardest to sit with, isn't it? It's certainly the part I find most difficult – the surrender which says that yes, I'll *do* my best, but that I don't actually *know* best. We're supposed to find comfort in the fact that, as believers, we know who does.

Surrendering our worry isn't the same as stopping our work. I hope that this book has shown just how significant our work in this world is. We are called to it, whatever work looks like for you in this current season. But what if real self-care meant taking Jesus at his word, when he says in Matthew 6:33: 'But seek first his kingdom and his righteousness, and all these things will be given to you as well.'

He's not our last resort, he's the author and perfecter of our faith (see Hebrews 12), and the good work he's started in us, he *will* bring to completion. We might wish he'd hurry up a bit, and we might even question whether he's actually heard what we've asked, but the truth about real self-care is thinking about soul and spirit *as well* as body, and casting our cares on to him before piling anything else on top of our already crowded lives. Any of those fixes (and some of them are good, don't get me wrong), are only ever going to be temporary. Let's look towards him who is eternal.

Food for thought

1   How easy do you find it to pay attention to your thoughts, taking them captive? Take this next week to do what you can to notice your thoughts. What does this cause you to note?

2   When was the last time you took a 'me moment'? Whether it was five minutes for an uninterrupted hot drink, or an afternoon at the spa, can you think of when you last took any time out of your working day purely for yourself? Is this a regular practice for you? What would need to happen in order for it to be?

3   Being completely honest with yourself, how easy do you find it to 'let go and let God'? What parts of Matthew 6:25–34 do you find most challenging to comprehend? Why not set aside some time to pray in faith that you'll be able to surrender your worry to him?

Wellbeing over well-balanced: concluding reflection

'Wellbeing has so much more to do with your source than your circumstances.'

What God spoke to me in the pitch-black early hours is what he continues to remind me of when I look at areas of seeming hopelessness either outside or within myself. It's what brings me back to response as opposed to reaction. It's what reminds me to look up.

Wellbeing has been painted in an over-glamorised light.

If a human being can't be well without buying something, what does that mean for those who can't afford it?

If a human being can't be well without positive thoughts and 'good vibes only', what does that mean for those with debilitating mental health challenges?

If a human being can't be well without belonging to a particular people or place, what does that mean for those who didn't win the postcode lottery?

Even my description of wellbeing – 'holistic health, hope and happiness, which reflects and acts on the past, present and future' – is flawed. We're not all healthy, we're not all happy and sometimes we can't even be hopeful. However, I hope this book has given you some tangible ways in which you might begin to access those things for yourself through reflection and action, but also, and most importantly, given you an understanding of how and why your wellbeing is about someone much greater than all your good will and good works combined.

Perhaps, as you've read this book, you've found yourself asking questions about whether Jesus truly is the answer for so much. Where are those questions leading you now? My hope is that you'll be led to want to further lean into him and learn more. My hope is that you'll realise that he meets you exactly where you are today and longs for you to let him hold your arms up where you've become too tired to manage.

One definition of balance is 'stability or steadiness due to the equilibrium prevailing between all the forces of any system' (Oxford English Dictionary). Work–life balance, therefore, firstly assumes that you want a balance between your work and the rest of your life, and then wrongly offers you the idea that this is something you can obtain by doing X or Y. Don't get me wrong, there will be days in your life which feel blissfully balanced. But what of those days which feel anything but?

Work–life wellbeing, however, asks you to check in with yourself. It questions what season you're currently in and acknowledges that if you're sprinting towards a deadline at work right now, you may well have a pile of laundry you've not gotten around to or vast amounts of unanswered WhatsApp messages from friends and family awaiting your reply. If you're in a season of healing and recovery, you may have concerned colleagues checking in or perhaps even slightly on-edge managers longing for you to reply to their emails and return to work.

The plates won't always spin perfectly at the same time. But maybe that's because you're not a circus act. You're a human being and not a human doing.

While people might not always understand the way in which you live your life, or perhaps it's you who doesn't understand why life is unfolding for you the way that it is right now, you can rest assured that your creator has a plan.

What would it take to liberate ourselves from the need to understand everything?

What would it take to liberate ourselves from explaining our ways to those committed to misunderstanding us?

What would it take for us to truly trust?

If right now you're not feeling especially well-rested, well-nourished and well-presented, I hope you know that you can still be well, no matter who or what might be telling you otherwise. It may not be immediate. It won't look perfect, and it won't look the way it does for your neighbour. But it can at least be right for you, right now, while you work out what's next.

In one of my earlier ventures within my previous coaching business, I'd sign off my emails with the phrase, 'If you want to go further, you have to dig deeper.' It's as true now as it was then. There is no place you can go (physically, mentally or emotionally) where God can't meet you. As you dig deeper in understanding this truth, I pray that you'll be met once more with the maker of heaven and earth and that you'll know the truest of transformations as a result.

I close with the prayer Paul prayed for the Ephesian church:

> I pray that out of his glorious riches he may strengthen you with power through his Spirit in your inner being, so that Christ may dwell in your hearts through faith. And I pray that you, being rooted and established in love, may have power, together with all the Lord's holy people, to grasp how wide and long and high and deep is the love of Christ, and to know this love that surpasses knowledge – that you may be filled to the measure of all the fullness of God.
> EPHESIANS 3:16–19

Keep going. Keep growing.

Notes

1   Julianne Holt-Lunstad, Timothy B. Smith and J. Bradley Layton, 'Social relationships and mortality risk: a meta-analytic review', *PLoS Med* 7(7) (2010).

2   Matthew W. Gallagher and Shane J. Lopez (eds), *The Oxford Handbook of Hope* (Oxford University Press, 2018), p. 134.

3   Alia J. Crum, Peter Salovey and Shawn Achor, 'Rethinking stress: the role of mindsets in determining the stress response', *Journal of Personality and Social Psychology* 104(4) (2013), pp. 716 33.

4   Matthew Kelly, *The Long View* (Beacon Publishing, 2014), p. 2.

5   Andrew Huberman, 'The science of gratitude and how to build a gratitude practice', Huberman Lab podcast, **hubermanlab.com/episode/the-science-of-gratitude-and-how-to-build-a-gratitude-practice**.

6   Cyril Northcote Parkinson, 'Parkinson's Law', *The Economist*, 19 November 1955, accessible online: **economist.com/news/1955/11/19/parkinsons-law**.

7   Jim Collins and Jerry Porras, *Built to Last: Successful habits of visionary companies* (HarperBusiness, 1994), chapter 5.

8   Lysa TerKeurst, *The Best Yes: Making wise decisions in the midst of endless demands* (Thomas Nelson, 2014), p. 21.

9   Daniel G. Amen, *Change Your Brain, Change Your Life*, revised and expanded edition (Little Brown Book Group, 2016), p. 25.

10 Francis Adams (ed.), *The Genuine Works of Hippocrates*, volume 2 (William Wood and Company, 1886), p. 345.

Journal pages

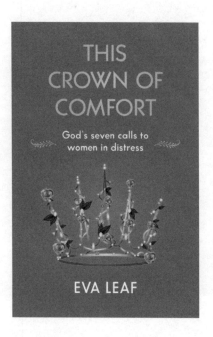

God deeply cares for those of us who are broken and hurt. And just as he helped his beloved Jerusalem find healing in her brokenness, he does the same for us. For he cried out seven double imperatives to her in the book of Isaiah, seven steps to restore her to wholeness, and he cries out the same to us. But he doesn't begin by scolding us; instead, he comforts. His first double imperative is, 'Comfort, comfort,' despite what has happened in our lives.

This Crown of Comfort
God's seven calls to women in distress
Eva Leaf
978 0 80039 208 3 £9.99

brfonline.org.uk

Some women of the Hebrew scriptures are well known, but many others are barely remembered. Even when they are, we often don't pause on them long enough to think about what we might learn from them. *Unveiled*, written with frankness and humour and illustrated with striking artwork from a young Oxford-based artist, explores the stories of 40 women in 40 days. Each reflection ends with a short application to everyday life, guidance for further thought and a prayer.

Unveiled
Women of the Old Testament and the choices they made
Reflections by Clare Hayns and artwork by Micah Hayns
978 0 80039 072 0 £14.99

brfonline.org.uk

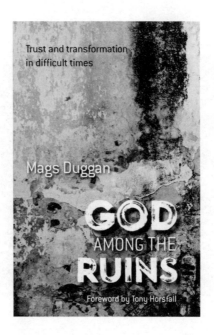

It takes courage to hope; to stand in our confusion and grief and still to believe that 'God is not helpless among the ruins'. Guided by Habakkuk and his prophetic landmarks, we are drawn on a reflective journey through the tangled landscape of bewildered faith, through places of wrestling and waiting, and on into the growth space of deepened trust and transformation. As you read, discover for yourself the value and practice of honest prayer, of surrender, of silence and listening, and of irrepressible hoping.

God Among the Ruins
Trust and transformation in difficult times
Mags Duggan
978 0 85746 575 7 £8.99

brfonline.org.uk

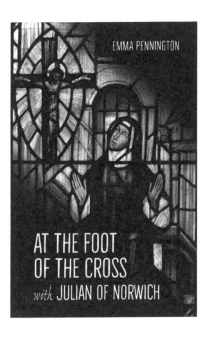

'All shall be well, and all shall be well, and all manner of thing shall be well.' This quote may be all that many people know of Julian of Norwich, an anchoress from the fourteenth century. This book seeks to bring to a popular readership a devotional engagement with Julian's work. Each chapter centres on one aspect or image from Julian's Revelation, which seeks to make the events of the Passion present to the reader's imagination. The commentary incorporates reflection, the biblical narrative and Julian's subsequent teachings to create a meditation that enables the reader to linger on the wonder of the cross, ending with a prayer that leads to silence and a thought or verse to carry into daily life.

At the Foot of the Cross with Julian of Norwich
Emma Pennington
978 0 85746 519 1 £9.99

brfonline.org.uk

Ministries

Inspiring people of all ages to grow in Christian faith

BRF Ministries is the home of Anna Chaplaincy, Living Faith, Messy Church and Parenting for Faith

---

As a charity, our work would not be possible without fundraising and gifts in wills.
To find out more and to donate,
visit brf.org.uk/give or call +44 (0)1235 462305